UNDERSTANDING MARGE PIERCY

UNDERSTANDING CONTEMPORARY AMERICAN LITERATURE

Matthew J. Bruccoli, Founding Editor

Linda Wagner-Martin, Series Editor

UNDERSTANDING

MARGE PIERCY

Donna M. Bickford

THE UNIVERSITY OF
SOUTH CAROLINA PRESS

Published by the University of South Carolina Press
Columbia, South Carolina 29208

www.sc.edu/uscpress

Manufactured in the United States of America

28 27 26 25 24 23 22 21 20 19
10 9 8 7 6 5 4 3 2 1

Library of Congress Cataloging-in-Publication Data
can be found athttp://catalog.loc.gov/.

ISBN 978-1-61117-952-1 (hardback)
ISBN 978-1-61117-953-8 (ebook)

“Stories make patterns where otherwise there would be chaos.”
Marge Piercy, “Port Huron Conference Statement”

CONTENTS

SERIES EDITOR'S PREFACE

The Understanding Contemporary American Literature series was founded by the estimable Matthew J. Bruccoli (1931–2008), who envisioned these volumes as guides or companions for students as well as good nonacademic readers, a legacy that will continue as new volumes are developed to fill in gaps among the nearly one hundred series volumes published to date and to embrace a host of new writers only now making their marks on our literature.

As Professor Bruccoli explained in his preface to the volumes he edited, because much influential contemporary literature makes special demands, "the word *understanding* in the titles was chosen deliberately. Many willing readers lack an adequate understanding of how contemporary literature works; that is, of what the author is attempting to express and the means by which it is conveyed." Aimed at fostering this understanding of good literature and good writers, the criticism and analysis in the series provide instruction in how to read certain contemporary writers—explicating their material, language, structures, themes, and perspectives— and facilitate a more profitable experience of the works under discussion.

In the twenty-first century Professor Bruccoli's prescience gives us an avenue to publish expert critiques of significant contemporary American writing. The series continues to map the literary landscape and to provide both instruction and enjoyment. Future volumes will seek to introduce new voices alongside canonized favorites, to chronicle the changing literature of our times, and to remain, as Professor Bruccoli conceived, contemporary in the best sense of the word.

Linda Wagner-Martin, Series Editor

ACKNOWLEDGMENTS

Sara Ahmed writes that "some feminists might even begin their feminist lives living in books" (17). I was one of these feminists; I came to feminism through literature. It is not the only or necessarily the best way, but it's the way I came. More specifically, it was the revolutionizing experience of reading Marge Piercy's novel *Vida* followed by other novels by her and other contemporary feminist writers that helped me begin to understand feminism and to fully claim it as part of my identity. It has been a great joy to continue to read and think about her work and to have the privilege of introducing my students to it. Most importantly, I offer my thanks and gratitude to Marge Piercy and hope she feels I have done justice to her prolific creativity and imagination.

I wrote about some of Piercy's novels in my dissertation. It may take a village to raise a child, but it takes a dissertation committee and its constructive critique to make a dissertation worth reading. I was fortunate to have the guidance of the late Dana Shugar, Mary Cappello, Jean Walton, Rosie Pegueros, Clemente White, Mario Trubiano, and Stephen Barber throughout that process. Mary, Jean, and Rosie have continued to be enthusiastic supporters of my career and, more importantly, dear friends.

This manuscript benefited greatly from the gift of a week-long writing residency at Wildacres where I was able to craft a mass of notes into an actual first draft. Thanks to the staff at Wildacres for their support and interest in my work, and to Randi Davenport for recommending that I apply for the residency.

My deep thanks to Dr. Linda Wagner-Martin, who has been an important mentor and supporter through many stages of my career. I was introduced to Linda's impactful scholarship in graduate school; it was a humbling experience later in my life to become her friend and colleague. Her invitation to write this book was incredibly affirming.

Just as Piercy writes about a multitude of strong women, I owe debts of gratitude to the strong women in my family who have nurtured, encouraged, validated, and loved me. My mother, Irene Rash, and my sisters Susan Bickford and Barbara Jean Bickford Wilcox Donow are vibrant exemplars of what it means to engage fully in life, to savor the joys and swim through the challenges, and to make thoughtful and intentional choices. Their husbands and children, Greg McAvoy, Les Donow, Earl Wilcox, Nathan Wilcox, and Benjamin McAvoy-Bickford have enriched my life immensely. Special thanks to Susan for reading the manuscript at a critical point in its development and for providing targeted and generative feedback.

We are all enmeshed in webs of love, friendship, and learning. I am lucky to be part of multiple intersecting networks. Thanks to Robin Dare, Janet Hagen, Anne Mitchell Whisnant, Randi Davenport, Cookie Newsom, and other colleagues and friends who have been and who continue to be significant parts of my life and my community.

I appreciate the support of the Dickinson College Research and Development Committee in providing supplemental funding for this project.

CHAPTER 1

Understanding Marge Piercy

Love, nature, politics, Judaism, family (blood and built), relationships, gardens, activism, community, cats—each of these is interwoven throughout Marge Piercy's work and life. Piercy (b. 1936) is one of the most astute U.S. novelists and poets currently writing. Notably prolific, she has published seventeen novels, nineteen books of poetry, a memoir, and collections of essays and short stories; yet, she remains undervalued in the literary establishment and unknown by many readers. Piercy confronts complicated issues of power, identity, and privilege—gender, race, sexuality, socioeconomic class, disability, age, nationalism, militarism, corporate hegemony—with a lucidity and lyricism not always found in contemporary fiction. Piercy began publishing her work in the 1960s, and her decades-long career continues to encompass the major post–World War II social movements and changing social mores.

Piercy's biography is as rich and varied as that of any of her characters. She grew up in a working-class family in Detroit. Her mother, Bert Bunnin Piercy, was Jewish; her father, Robert Piercy, was not. In her memoir, *Sleeping with Cats,* Piercy writes that her "father's family was casually and relentlessly anti-Semitic" (20). Her parents were "ill suited" (31) in Piercy's estimation, and their relationship was rocky: "They were always at war, and I was one of their battlegrounds" (14). Although Robert Piercy was not physically violent with his wife, he did hit and kick his daughter (36). He wanted a son, and so Piercy was "never satisfactory"; she felt that her father never really loved her and that she did not and could not please him. He had a stronger relationship with Piercy's half-brother, the child of her mother's earlier marriage, who was quite a bit older than Piercy (14).

Piercy comes from "a long line of storytelling women" (*Sleeping* 13). She had a strong bond with her maternal grandmother, Hannah, who lived with her family during the summer. Hannah was an Orthodox Jew who, Piercy said, "gave me my religious education" (Templin 4). Piercy's mother often played word games with her; she credits her mother with teaching her to observe closely, a practice that benefits all writers. However, once Piercy entered puberty, the relationship between her and her mother became much more difficult (*Sleeping* 10), and it was not until the later years of her mother's life that they grew close again. The unexpected and sudden death of her mother was a very difficult time for Piercy.

Piercy's family struggled economically. She wore hand-me-down clothes; there was not money for medical or dental care; and often there was minimal food available. Still, her family was very invested in identifying as middle class, seeing owning a car and a house as important class markers. In the poem "My mother's novel" from *The Moon Is Always Female,* Piercy describes her mother as "a small woman of large longings" who "married her way / at length into the solid workingclass" (8, 15). Piercy's mother was a housewife and worked "incessantly" (*Sleeping* 15). In her writing and in her own life, Piercy consistently insists on recognizing that domestic, emotional labor is work.

Growing up in the fifties was very difficult for Piercy. The culture, social practices, and societal expectations combined to be "a mutilating time to grow up female" ("Through the Cracks" 126). She could not find "images of a life I considered good or useful or dignified. . . . Nowhere could I find a community to heal myself to in struggle." Piercy says to John Rodden: "It feels nutty when it's only you. You're regarded as insane. It isn't until there exists some kind of framework in which to hold onto the insights [feminist consciousness] that it makes any sense. To be concerned with these things by yourself was, in the 1950s, to be a little crazy" (137). It was not until the sixties that she was able to think, "'I might be useful, I might speak and be heard, listen and receive'" ("Through the Cracks" 127).

Piercy has frequently challenged the complaints of other writers about the difficulty of writing, acknowledging that writing "is frequently hard" but that "it beats anything else I was ever paid for, and sometimes to this day I remain astonished I am paid for writing poems and making up stories" ("What I Do When I Write" 25). She has also asserted, "I like to write. I'm probably unusual in that I am a writer who actually likes to write" (Lyons 340). She has also commented about the difficulty of making a living as a writer: "You don't get paid much. . . . I live two-thirds off my speaking and teaching gigs" (Lyons 333). This also has an impact on her future, as "I won't have a pension" ("Our Money").

Piercy was an avid reader throughout her childhood and adolescence. Weekly library visits with her mother gave her access to books that began to give her a sense that "my life might be different, wider than my mother's" (*Sleeping* 32).

She reflects that "perhaps I was looking for role models, for lives to try on mentally" (48). When Piercy was fifteen, her family moved to a house large enough that she was able to have a room of her own; it was with that new-found privacy that she began to write ("The Lunar Cycle" 63; "An Interview with Denise Wagner" 204). As Piercy describes it, "I wanted to be a writer and had been turning out both poetry and prose since I was fifteen and got a room of my own with a door that shut" ("The City as Battleground" 168).[1] In that room, she has written, "I became who I was to be" (*Sleeping* 69).

Piercy was the first person in her family to attend college. Her parents opposed her desire to pursue higher education and "mistrusted college and higher education for a woman" (*Sleeping* 92). Her mother wanted her to have an office job, because Bert "could not imagine any higher calling for a woman than to have a nice secretarial job in an office with middle-class men to flirt with, wearing nice clothes to work and bringing home a little money" ("Things" 95). Their lack of support meant that Piercy financed her own education from her savings from jobs she held as a teenager, from scholarships she earned and from jobs she held during her undergraduate years. Piercy earned her B.A. in 1957 from the University of Michigan, from which she received several Hopwood awards and where she has donated her papers.

After college, Piercy traveled to France with Michel Schiff, a French physicist who she then married. Her parents refused to attend the wedding, which Piercy "could not understand" (*Sleeping* 112). She apparently assumed that they would value Schiff as a good partner for their daughter, since he was an educated, professional man from a comfortable class status. She earned her M.A. from Northwestern University in 1958. They divorced in 1959. In 1962 she married her second husband, Robert Shapiro, a computer scientist; they moved to Wellfleet on Cape Cod in the early 1970s. At Shapiro's instigation but with Piercy's eventual agreement, part of the time they were together they shared an open marriage—each of them free to engage in relationships with others as they chose. Open marriage was a political and personal strategy to attempt to reject the patriarchal nuclear family, and often these secondary lovers became part of their family. Piercy and Shapiro divorced in 1980, however, when their primary relationship soured.

After being friends and then romantically involved for several years, Piercy and Ira Wood married in 1982. Wood is younger than Piercy, something she has called "a tradition in my mother's family" since her mother and her aunt both had younger husbands (*Sleeping* 4). Piercy has suggested that "younger men in our society at present have less rigid expectations about sex roles than do men my age or older" (Lyons 343), a sentiment also voiced by Natalie in *Vida* (158). Piercy and Wood have continued to live on Cape Cod where they have maintained extensive food and flower gardens; Piercy has estimated that they "grow 90% of our own vegetables, can, freeze, dehydrate" (Barnat). They co-founded and ran the publishing house Leapfrog Press for several years, they have co-written a play and a novel, and they teach writing workshops together. They share many interests, Piercy has written, "but the core of our relationship has always been communication and sex, the exchange of words and the joining of our bodies" (*Sleeping* 8). Early on in her life, Piercy decided not to have children and has never regretted that decision (339); she observes that most of her mother's generation of Bunnins "were childless by choice" (26). Piercy has, however, almost always had cats. In fact, she says her "life has a spine of cats" (4), indicating their centrality in her world.

Piercy almost died as a child, after bouts of German measles and rheumatic fever (*Sleeping* 28). She has continued to experience health challenges throughout her life, exacerbated by lack of access to medical care early in her life due to poverty. She has suggested that "part of my health problems are a result of my childhood, and part from my political involvement—especially being gassed" (Lyons 340). She became quite ill during her time in New York with lung problems she attributes both to years of smoking and being gassed frequently in protests and demonstrations ("Afterthoughts" 317–18). More recently, she has had eye surgery and two knee replacements.

For much of Piercy's emerging and early adulthood, she worked a variety of low-wage jobs in order to support herself, rising early in the morning to write before she left for work. She has described the motivation of economic necessity: "in order to survive, I worked as a secretary, I was an artist's model, switchboard operator, all that shit" (Godwin 29). She has always been politically active; her political commitments were also time-consuming and for many years she fit her writing into the spaces around these other activities. Early on, she was very involved in anti–Vietnam War activism, with Students for a Democratic Society (SDS) and with the North American Congress on Latin America (NACLA). Piercy was also one of the founders of Movement for a Democratic Society (MDS), which she described both as "an adult chapter" of SDS (*Sleeping* 177) and as "an early form of NACLA" (Godwin 29).

The sexism embedded throughout the New Left led Piercy to embrace women's liberation (*Sleeping* 204–5). *Leviathan,* a journal founded to explore issues of concern to MDS, published her essay "The Grand Coolie Dam" in November 1969; it was republished in a collection of feminist essays in 1970. Piercy called out the sexism endemic in the Movement in her opening question: "The Movement is supposed to be for human liberation: how come the condition of women inside it is no better than outside?" (421). She noted the exploitation of women's labor within the movement, the silencing and ignoring of women's voices, and the posturing of men to maintain or enhance their standing within the Movement. Piercy also critiqued Movement strategies, noting their lack of success in "learning how to reach all kinds of people" (426) and pointing out that the "monstrosities of jargon" in Movement publications "fail to make our politics lucid to people on a level where they can become autonomous political thinkers and doers" (427). This issue surfaces in *Vida* when Vida and Joel want to act rather than write yet another position paper that will not resonate with the general public (272, 277). Piercy acknowledged her past internalization and acceptance of the male structures and male domination of the Movement, refusing the suggestion that "women's liberation is a secondary issue, to be dealt with after the war is won" (437).

Piercy continued to work in the Movement, but also began to ground herself in feminist activism. She organized consciousness-raising sessions in a newly established Women's Center (*Sleeping* 205), helped start Cape Cod Women's Liberation (213), co-wrote *Getting Together: How to Start a Consciousness-Raising Group* with Jane Freeman, and was part of the Boston-based Bread and Roses (221). In the FAQ section of her website, she writes of her identification as a feminist: "I can't imagine not identifying strongly as a woman and not wanting things to be better and safer and more fun and less dangerous for myself and other women."

Piercy has continued to be engaged in activism and political struggles for social change. She participated in efforts to resist the recent wars in Iraq and Afghanistan and currently works to try to shut down the Pilgrim Nuclear Power Station, as well as being involved in other local community issues on Cape Cod, particularly those related to the environment. She recently disclosed that after the 2016 Presidential election, "I can't seem to write anything but political poems since the election . . . Writing political poems requires just as much craft as writing poems bout [*sic*] irises or a lover. But I just can't get my mind around any other subject yet" ("Busy Week, Snip, Etc."). Many of her activist experiences and commitments inform her writing.

Piercy has lived in many places in addition to Detroit, including Chicago, Boston, San Francisco, and New York. She has deeply inhabited cityscapes and landscapes and they have flowed into her work. Lauren Belfer has written of *Sex Wars* that one aspect of the plot line "becomes merely an extended opportunity for Piercy to explore still more neighborhoods of the city." Piercy has acknowledged, "the sense of place is extremely important to me in being able to enter a character's past or present" ("Life of Prose"). When Piercy moved to the Cape, carving out dedicated time for writing was a priority for her; Piercy noted that "from the time I arrived on the Cape, one of the things I chose explicitly was to put my writing first" (*Sleeping* 218). She built friendships with many other notable writers, including Denise Levertov and Adrienne Rich, and Piercy particularly cherished the ability to talk with them about writing (*Sleeping* 225); of Rich, Piercy noted that "I used to see her and have lunch with her on a regular basis" ("Trying to Calm Down"). Piercy also blogs frequently on her website (margepiercy.com) where she has shared details of life on the Cape, gardening adventures, accounts of hosting and entertaining guests, cat exploits, what she is reading, her political views and analyses, works in progress, and other musings.

For much of her career Piercy has also selectively reviewed the work of others, particularly other women writers. She has regarded this as "a duty"; to Piercy, reviewing "feels more like sharing the life-support jobs in a household than like creativity" ("Mirror Image" 208). She has viewed it as a necessity, "something you must put back in the movement, something you must do for others" (209). Piercy told Peggy Friedmann and Ruthann Robson, "I think of it as a service activity" ("An Interview" 137). Because "there's so much women's work that doesn't get reviewed at all," Piercy has maintained that "reviewing is something that I just have to do" ("Interview with Karla Hammond" 37). In recent years, however, the activity of reviewing other writers has become less necessary for her: "I think critiquing other people's work is something I did a lot of between thirty and sixty years of age, but it's not a priority now. I have too much to do in the time left me" (Casper). Perhaps feeling that she has paid her dues in this arena has led her to be able to concentrate fully on her own writing. But it is also an economic decision; as she reminded Monica Casper, "I live off my writing, which means I am very busy writing, giving readings, speeches, workshops."

Piercy has been mentoring other writers through her annual juried poetry workshops and through the workshops she and Wood offer around the country. She has also been remarkably consistent in the public advice she shares with aspiring writers. When Mary Mackey asked what was "the single most important thing anyone who wants to be a serious writer should know," Piercy responded: "If you want to write short stories, read short stories. Don't read a book about writing short stories" (Mackey). In an interview with Michael Luzzi she said, "to young writers all you can say is read and write and read and write and read and write" (151). In response to a question by Dana Barnat, Piercy advised, "read, read, read. . . . Look at the craft. . . . Learn to revise." In her poem "For the Young Who Want To," Piercy is quite definitive and pointed in her statement: "The real writer is one / who really writes" (31–32).

Although Piercy's work is clearly inspired by and grounded in feminism, it is not the feminist caricature embodied in some mainstream media (shrill, man-hating, sex-hating, and so on), but a more complex, nuanced, and accurate image of feminism that calls attention to its benefits for men as well as for women, and also acknowledges and critiques power struggles between women. As a *Booklist* review of her novel *Small Changes* described, "Piercy is not a simple proselytizer; she writes about authentic people—young men and women whose small changes are really landmarks of inner strength or loss" (633). Susan Mernit asserted that "Piercy has consistently sought to show how personal history is shaped by political beliefs and social conditions" (18). Piercy noted that she writes "character-centered fiction" ("An Interview with Allison Platt" 177) and novels where readers want to know "what then" ("Mirror Images" 211); fiction, including hers, she said, "is still about pattern in human life" (211). Far from being a superficial fictional cover for feminist ideology, Piercy's novels are skillfully developed, full of compelling plots and engaging characters.

Piercy's fiction makes important contributions to literary representations of social movements—including feminism and the anti-war movement—but, pigeonholing her writing as just political fiction is too facile and limiting. Mernit argued in her review of *Fly Away Home* that Piercy's work is evidence "that artistic creation is not incompatible with political commitment" (18). Piercy noted the double standard that motivates those critiques: "People tend to define 'political' or 'polemical' in terms of what is not congruent with their ideas. . . . The defense of the status quo is as political as an attack on it" ("Interview with Karla Hammond" 34). That loaded description ignores the ways in which her work engages with a wide range of contemporary American experiences, and the ways in which she has used specific stories to illuminate overarching concerns. This perception of her work is likely responsible for the absence of sustained attention to Piercy's writing.

Although Nan Nowik called Piercy one of our "most prolific and important contemporary women writers" (208), the perception that Piercy's work is only valuable politically, rather than as literature, has impacted her ability to achieve mainstream recognition. As Piercy commented, although readers in the general public and academics who "produce interesting criticism" value her work, the literary establishment has generally failed to recognize it. Piercy observed that she is "a writer not ever part of the establishment" ("What I Do When I Write" 26). She has predicted: "I see no sign I will be recognized in that way until I am dead" (*Sleeping* 339). Piercy has also discussed the benefits of publishing for a broad audience: "I want to reach people who don't go into bookstores. So that means mass paperback is very important to me." She added: "I also want to reach people who do go into bookstores" ("Interview with Karla Hammond" 25), indicating a desire to be read by the widest range and number of people possible.

In many of Piercy's novels and poems, she has given voice to multiple perspectives and used flashbacks to provide the personal and family histories of her characters. These narrative choices help the reader to see how characters have been shaped, both by embodying and resisting family and societal belief systems and practices. Piercy's work consistently explores the daily lives of fully developed individuals, presenting their decisions, challenges, and joys against a rich swath of contemporary history.

Because of Piercy's productivity, there is no way that one book could adequately consider the totality of her work. This study groups together novels dealing with related themes and closes by examining Piercy's poetry.

CHAPTER 2

Small Changes, Vida, Braided Lives

Societal Changes

The rapidly changing social, political, and cultural mores of the 1960s and 70s made it seem possible to inhabit the world in different ways, or even to build a new world. There were strong connections between the activists involved in the civil rights movement, the anti-war movement, the New Left, and second-wave feminism; many activists, of course, were involved in multiple movements with overlapping allegiances. Many future second-wave feminists began their political activism during the struggle for civil rights as they journeyed South to participate in sit-ins and to help register black voters. As activist and scholar Sheila Tobias noted in *Faces of Feminism,* her 1997 narrative of the development and subsequent activities of the women's movement, the "mass migration of northern students to the South had a searing effect on the white women students who had volunteered" (77). Rachel Blau DuPlessis and Ann Snitow agreed that "the formative and galvanizing source for the women's movement was the Civil Rights movement" which "had already made the case that justice in the United States would require fundamental social change" (6).

Women also became engaged in protests against the Vietnam War and/or joined Students for a Democratic Society (SDS) or other leftist movements which worked to end oppression in multiple arenas. Tobias noted the irony of SDS and the New Left practices; the organizations were saturated by sexism and male privilege at the same time as they worked for racial equity, the eradication of the draft, and other social justice issues.[1] In 1965, Casey Hayden and Mary King called out this hypocrisy, writing that "many people who are very hip to the implications of the racial caste system, even people in the movement, don't seem to be able to see the sexual caste system" (22). An SDS national convention was briefly disrupted by a group of women who wanted to call attention to sexism within the movement; the women were booed by men as well as by other women, demonstrating that patriarchal indoctrination did not just impact men's thoughts and behaviors.

Both Tobias and Estelle Freedman described some distinctions between the focus and strategies of different factions within second-wave feminism. Feminists "worked for social change with the rare urgency that comes from believing in the immediate possibility of a fundamentally different world" (DuPlessis and Snitow 7), but the goals, strategies, and tactics differed. Liberal feminists were involved in electoral politics, attempting to change unfair laws and policies. The women's liberation movement, on the other hand, "questioned the liberal feminist goal of integrating women into male power structures" (Freedman 87). Their aim was for more radical societal changes, and their analyses included, among other things, "the deconstruction of everyday life" (DuPlessis and Snitow 13). Radical feminists questioned everything, making apparent the invisible assumptions embedded in societal practices and institutions. Why were women almost solely responsible for housework and why were housework and other care work so undervalued? How have the accepted responsibilities for public versus private domains limited and constrained women? Why were women paid less than men and why were female-dominated professions paid so little? Why were women considered to be working for "pin money" even if they were supporting or helping to support their families? Why did men control the checkbooks and make the financial decisions for their families? Why were women expected to accommodate male sexual desire often without regard for their own desire or pleasure? New words were coined for experiences like marital rape and sexual harassment—words that described behaviors so normalized and pervasive that they had been unquestioned for decades. Piercy's activism has been most closely aligned with this latter trajectory of feminist work and it is easy to see how her feminist allegiances and practices inform her writing.

The term "second-wave feminism" comes from a conceptual lens that has frequently been invoked to describe the trajectory of U.S. feminism. In this metaphor, the first wave encompasses the suffrage movement, the second wave refers to the women's liberation movement which began in the 1960s and 1970s, and the third wave applies to contemporary feminism and is generally understood to have begun in the 1990s. The wave metaphor has been critiqued by scholars including Nancy Hewitt, who argued that this metaphor implies that feminist work "is contained in discrete and separate waves, while in reality such movements overlapped and intertwined" (5), and (erroneously), that "the decades excluded from the waves . . . are assumed to be feminist-free zones" (5).

Hewitt went on to point out that framing feminist work/history in waves often makes invisible the variety of issues being addressed in any given moment, ignoring, for example, the ways in which women of color were involved in feminist activism in the 1960s and 1970s, or the global connections between feminists throughout centuries of U.S. feminist practice (5). Hokulani K. Aikau, Karla A. Erickson, and Jennifer L. Pierce have also challenged the usefulness of the metaphor, noting that "it collapses differences between generations of feminists and their intellectual work" (5) and "flattens . . . the complexity of theories and concepts produced in particular historical moments" (5).

Lisa Jervis denounced this conceptual framework even more categorically: "We've reached the end of the wave terminology's usefulness. . . . [it] has become shorthand that invites intellectual laziness, an escape hatch from the hard work of distinguishing between core beliefs and a cultural movement" (14). But even with her strong denunciation of the wave language, Jervis recognized generational differences in some cohorts of feminists that are based on lack of knowledge and information about each other: "Here's what we all need to recognize so that we can move on: Those in their twenties and thirties who don't see their concerns reflected in the feminism of their elders are ignorant of their history; those in their fifties and beyond who think that young women aren't politically active, or active enough, or active around the right issues, don't know where to look" (17).

Despite the flaws in and limitations of the metaphor, it can also be a convenient framework, however partial and contingent. Piercy has identified herself as "a woman active in the Second Wave of feminism" ("Sex Wars: The Writing Of"). She also clearly recognized the importance of what has been labeled the first wave of feminism, as evidenced in *Sex Wars.* Piercy has resonated strongly with third-wave feminism, too, and she was particularly struck by the Riot Grrrl phenomenon,[2] dedicating her book *Early Grrrl: The Early Poems of Marge Piercy* (1999) to them and writing in the book's dedication of how "the grrrls" have inspired her. The utility of the waves, however, in informing Piercy's activism and understanding some aspects of her work should not be taken as a rigid framework for interpretative purposes.

In *Notes from an Incomplete Revolution,* Meredith Mahan succinctly described the issues women's liberation has insisted be considered and analyzed: "What it means to be a woman; what it means to be a man; what it means to love one, or the other, or both; what equality might look like; what power is and who should have it and how it should be wielded" (x). Three of Piercy's novels—*Small Changes, Vida,* and *Braided Lives*—chronicle the decades in which these questions were wrestled with vigorously. Beth and Miriam in *Small Changes* find their sexual identities and search for work they enjoy and find fulfilling. Vida struggles with the sexism of revolutionary movements to establish herself as a full and equal participant. Jill and Donna in *Braided Lives* figure out what it means to be female in the 1950s and 1960s. All of these stories take place against the social and political landscape of their time: these three novels particularly illuminate the interactions between the civil rights movement, the New Left, the anti-war movement, and the beginnings of second-wave feminism. Through interconnected themes, the novels portray individuals who experiment with new ways of living in families and communities, embodying a resistance to conventional gender and sex roles, ultimately hoping to create more freedom and flexibility for women and men. The narrators strive to imagine how to live a meaningful life where, in the title of one of Piercy's poems, one might "be of use" (*To Be Of Use* 49). As Bonnie Lyons commented to Piercy in an interview, "usefulness is clearly a major theme in your work" (329).

Braided Lives begins in the 1950s and is, in Piercy's own synopsis: "about two friends who go to college from working-class families and work out their destinies in the world of rigid sex roles and Freudian orthodoxy of the years before the women's movement had made abortion legal and provided alternatives to women besides 'marry or die.' It is also a portrait of the artist as a feisty young girl, candid, independent, street-wise, buffeted, and hard-tried by the prevailing mores and values of those conservative times" ("Mirror Images" 215–16).

Piercy's life experiences have seeped productively into most of her writing; however, she has acknowledged that *Braided Lives* is the most overtly autobiographical. She was quick to clarify that such an acknowledgment "is not to say that it is autobiography—it is far more novel than memoir" ("Marge Piercy" 280). Writing is a craft, and her novels and poems are never just unmediated, transparent reflections of reality, but are carefully and creatively molded and shaped.

The title *Braided Lives* alludes to the intersecting currents in the lives of many of the characters in the novel; as Judith Wilt noted, the lives most tightly braided together are Jill and her mother, and Jill and her cousin Donna (92). As a teenager, Jill's relationship with her mother, Pearl, is torturous—strained to the point that Jill thinks "I don't even remember what Mother and I quarreled about: it is a continual quarrel that began when I reached puberty" (5). Jill has carved out a bedroom for herself in the attic, which she sees as her "sanctuary" (19). This private space is important to her both as a space to retreat from Pearl and also as a place where she can feel autonomous, where she can write and be creative; it is "*my* room" (19), another allusion to Virginia Woolf's assertion in *A Room of One's Own* of the importance of private space to women artists.

When Jill one day comes home from school to find that her mother has painted the room "a shrieking yellow" (41) without her permission, she is furious both at the invasion of her privacy and at Pearl's attempts to put her imprimatur on Jill's space, constraining her independence.

Jill's efforts to define herself and her future as something—anything—other than what her mother embodies are met with Pearl's scorn, belittlement, and anger. In a rare generous moment, Jill realizes something about her mother's motives: "She is scared of the world and thinks if she punishes me first, I will be broken down enough to squeak through" (12). Here Jill recognizes that Pearl is trying, at least in part, to protect her. This brief moment of understanding, when Jill is able to acknowledge the good, albeit misguided, intention of at least some of Pearl's motivations, does little to negate the continual conflict between them.

Discussing Pearl's fear, Judith Wilt remarked: "Jill's mother sensed the danger as her daughter grew up rough, self-motivated, ambitious for education, mysteriously committed to the uncertain life of a writer and desirous of the rich and sometimes dangerous experiences that feed a writer's omnivorous imagination" (93).

Jill sees college as one way to escape both her mother and the future her mother plans for her, and her determination to go to college is rewarded by a scholarship to the University of Michigan. Pearl wants Jill to go to Wayne, a local college. It is only when they learn that Jill's cousin Donna has also won a scholarship to Michigan (and the two can room together—in a girl's dormitory with a curfew) that her parents relent and give their grudging permission.

Jill and Donna are both eager to leave home, go to college, and have a life as different from their parents as they can begin to imagine. Settling in at the university, Jill is deliriously happy at the chance to learn, cramming her mind full of information, reading voraciously, and sinking into the opportunity to write poetry. Donna goes on date after date, looking for the right man. Jill cannot understand why Donna adapts herself so quickly to the men she dates, a chameleon changing her tastes and conversation so the man she is with will approve of and desire her, whether she likes him or not. But it's the trend at that time, in a world where women measure their success, in large part, by whether they are attached to a man. Women transform themselves into whatever persona they think will result in being chosen by a man, a pattern Jill noticed as a teenager when she observed that "girls when they talk to boys become different" (21). These practices continue in her college friends to the extent that even their virginity magically disappears and reappears. Jill thinks tiredly, "I have a moment of seeing the whole dormitory as a minefield of sexual hypocrisy, all women lying to each other about what they are doing or not doing with boys they also lie to, because the boys lie to and about them" (123). It's a coping strategy, a technique designed to provide some space for women to act as they desire (or as their men desire) without facing social ostracism.

When Jill begins to date Mike, another poet, she finds herself conscious of trying to please him, the practice she is critical of in Donna. When Mike shows Jill one of his poems, she observes that, "carefully I proffer my reactions, grooming them to his pleasure" (101). Mike pushes her to say she loves him, but Jill is hesitant. What she has seen in relationships purportedly based on love, like that of her parents, are relationships that are full of manipulation and anger. Jill doesn't want that. She argues with Mike, remarking, "love is what stuck my parents together, gouging each other" (102). Jill doesn't want to jeopardize what she has fought so hard for—"a little freedom" (103). It's impossible for her to imagine both love and equality.

During spring vacation, Mike comes to meet Jill's parents, providing Pearl another opportunity to criticize Jill: Jill doesn't know how to act with a man; she doesn't know how to flirt. Jill is still mostly trying to resist falling into typically gendered patterns of behavior, insisting to Pearl, "I believe in being honest with men" (128). This is also part of Jill's determination to differentiate herself from her mother: "I don't want to live like my mother, I don't want to be like my mother" (196). In the absence of any alternative cultural models, Jill is trying to invent her own.

The fear of pregnancy and the consequences of getting pregnant are woven throughout this novel and drive the narrative forward. Piercy said that writing about illegal abortion "was the primary motive for writing the novel" (Rodden 140). Judith Wilt called it "a full-throated cry for abortion rights" (67). When Donna's first pregnancy scare comes in the middle of finals; Jill promises to help her find and finance an abortion. Her efforts at fund-raising causes a huge fight with Mike; jealous of the closeness between Donna and Jill, he refuses to pledge to contribute to an abortion fund if needed, announcing "I won't help finance murder" (160). Jill is shocked at his unyielding, moralistic attitude: "It's her body—don't you see that? She's no incubator" (160). Luckily, it turns out that Donna is not pregnant (this time), but Jill begins compiling information about doctors who will do abortions in the expectation that they will be needed in the future (283). In fact, in the pre-*Roe* era, women did create such lists; the information was necessary and useful to many women.

When Jill and Mike are both back in Detroit for the summer, her parents discover that they have been sleeping together, and they attempt to force Jill and Mike to marry (185). In the middle of this ongoing fracas and unremitting pressure, Jill discovers she is pregnant. Pearl confronts Jill with the calendar on which Jill notes her menstrual cycles, which makes clear that Jill has not had a period recently. Jill does not intend to tell Mike about the pregnancy and decides to have an abortion, an option her mother emphatically refuses, exhorting, "It's against the law. You can go to jail. Your father would kill me!" (209). Finally Pearl says "I'll tell you what to do . . . You'll have to do this for yourself" (209). Jill tries hot baths, laxatives, herbs, "jumping off porches"—but nothing works. Finally, Pearl says "We'll get you quinine and you take that and then the next day a mustard bath. If that fails you have to open the womb yourself" (215). In the end, Jill is forced to take this most extreme action and she comes close to dying. Mike is told that Jill has miscarried—in fact, he did not know she was pregnant—and by the time school begins again, their relationship is over.

When Donna fears she is pregnant again, this time as a result of a rape, Jill reflects on how vulnerable the inability to prevent pregnancy makes women: "I go through it every four months with some woman and I have gone through it with Donna before. How much money, what shall we do, who do you know, and will they do it and how much humiliation and pain will it cost and will they do it in time? At least on this occasion I am prepared" (370). This time Donna really is pregnant. Jill accompanies her to the abortion feeling lucky that "the abortion is performed in a house that is a clinic inside, clean and efficient" and that the abortionist "has the patient wait and recover on his premises to make sure no complications seem likely" (415). The fact that these minimal safety standards are noteworthy indicates the undesirable, unsanitary conditions in which many women at the time had abortions.

Women have always sought to control their own bodies, even at risk of punishment or death. While she is sitting with Donna after the procedure, Jill thinks of the reproductive history of the women in her family: "Buhbe had twelve children and at least five abortions; Mother three children, at least two abortions and a miscarriage that almost killed her. . . . So women have always done in all societies everywhere, with or without male knowledge or aid, with or without the help of official medicine and law" (415–16). Kerstin W. Shands wrote that "abortion is an issue that politicized Marge Piercy herself" (104), and the results of that are clearly visible in *Braided Lives*.

After college, Jill moves to New York; Donna and her husband, Peter, do as well. When Jill and Howie, her longtime childhood friend now in medical school at Columbia, become intimate and eventually decide to get married, they fly back to Michigan to tell their families. When Jill returns to her apartment after the trip, she discovers Donna's body; since "she died alone here hemorrhaging violently," it's clear to Jill that Donna must have had an abortion (529). Jill is distraught and furious: "Did she abort herself? But she had money. She must have found a doctor. Why didn't she tell me? Why?" (529).

As a way to cope with her grief, Jill starts a group to support women seeking abortions. First working with doctors and later learning to do the procedure themselves, they "provided the cheapest and safest abortions available" (548). When desperate women call, they use Donna's name as a code. Jill calculates that "three thousand women over the years remember Donna who got them out of trouble; who brought them better lives for themselves and the kids they had and could try to love" (548). Eventually "when abortion is finally legalized after "our demonstrations and pressure . . . Donna was retired" (548). Here Piercy gestures to the uncertainty and tenuousness of women's access to reproductive freedom as Jill muses "for how long?" How long will a Supreme Court decision allow women to make their own decisions about reproduction? It is a prescient question considering that immediately after *Roe* was decided, limitations and restrictions began to be placed on the right to choose an abortion; these efforts to overturn *Roe* or to circumvent it in some way have continued, most intensely at the state level.

Jill's strategy of finding a way to provide access to abortions is a reminder of the work of the Jane Collective, started in Chicago in the late 1960s. Using the name Jane as a code, a network of women involving "scores of volunteers" helped women seeking abortions, first by finding doctors to perform them, and then ultimately learning to perform abortions themselves. The Jane Collective also provided information about birth control, counseling, and support. As Lindsy Van Gelder wrote: "What had simply been a service to meet a need became a self-consciously political commitment to the larger concept of female empowerment" (83). This commitment to empowerment in relation to women's health, specifically, can also be seen in the *Our Bodies, Ourselves* movement,[3] which began during the second wave of feminism.

In addition to the themes of sex and its reproductive costs to women, Piercy concentrates on Jill's development as a writer. In college, Jill values her identity as a writer, asserting that "my poetry is one of the few parts of life where I feel brave" (65). She writes about things that are important to her, only to have them dismissed by her (male) English professor. He critiques one poem because of its focus on "the experiments of puberty," which he feels "should be kept to oneself" (64). During her involvement with Mike, it becomes quickly obvious that he takes only his own writing seriously, not hers. After they both participate in a public poetry reading, he demonstrates overt contempt, responding to one of her poems, "of course it's formless and silly. It isn't art, naturally" (153). During an argument later in their relationship, Mike targets her work, cruelly asserting that "most of what you write is just *merde*" and claiming that because he has "spent years thinking about aesthetics," he is somehow more authentic or talented as a writer (205).

Jill refuses to give up. In New York, she finds a series of part-time jobs, squeaking by financially to preserve time to write. She drinks in New York the same way she absorbed knowledge in college and finds that "the freedom to work ignites me. The best thing about being a writer is that I get to sit down and write" (461). Jill becomes involved in the cultural and political life of New York, attending demonstrations and literary events. After hearing Allen Ginsberg read his poetry, Jill has an epiphany about her own work: "it is possible to write with the whole entire live self . . . You can write your politics. You can actually write poems that say what you feel and think" (499). Piercy has remarked upon the impact Ginsberg had on her own work, saying both that he "liberated my imagination at a critical time" ("Afterthoughts" 305) and that he "broke open the world of writing for me ("Touched by Ginsburg" 63).

In *Braided Lives,* Piercy also addressed society's increasing attachment to and belief in Freudian psychotherapy, but with an intensely critical eye that recognized how it has been used to proscribe/control women's behavior. One of Donna and Jill's college dorm-mates, Theo, had been in therapy in New York before coming to college. She became sexually involved with her psychoanalyst because "I had sexual problems, he explained, that could only be worked out by him. On top" (107).[4] When Jill dates Peter, he is in therapy and tries to convince her to go to therapy by invoking Freudian concepts about women's sexuality: "You take yourself too seriously. All those compensation mechanisms because you're not fulfilling yourself as a woman." Jill is not at all convinced by this argument, recognizing that whatever she might share in therapy would be used against her: "I should go offer up my secrets to the enemy?" (283). Once Donna and Peter are married, Donna begins psychoanalysis, which she continues when they move to New York, saying of her therapist, "I worship him" (477). The therapist has decided that Donna's "fear of having children is related to [her] sexual identity problems" (478). Once she gets through therapy, she'll apparently be properly reconciled to her role as a woman and be ready to have children.

The control of women by men is a theme throughout the book. While at college, Jill muses, "All women are misfits, I think; we do not fit into this world without amputations" (108). The world is designed by and for men, who exert power over women to meet their needs. Women are forced to fit themselves into the spaces men permit them to occupy. Even Howie, who has been part of her life since high school and knows who she really is more fully than most people, expects Jill to put him, his career and his needs first, arguing "you can't marry me and do these things . . . I won't let you make a fool of me" (547). Jill and Howie end their sexual relationship when she realizes that he doesn't want "the me inside" (547). The final words of the novel relate to the necessity of openness and trust for a successful intimate relationship: "Freedom is a daily necessity like water, and we love most loyally and longest those who allow us at least occasionally to vanish and wander the curious night" (551). This seems like a much richer and more poetic rendition of: "If you love something, let it go. If it comes back to you, it's yours forever."

Many of the reviews of *Braided Lives* were very positive, recognizing elements of truth in the experiences Piercy portrayed. Vickie Leonard observed that, "this is the book of a feminist who can honestly face the brutality in our lives and can still maintain a gluttonous appetite for life" ("Braided Lives" 23). A *Publisher's Weekly* review noted, "While abortion is the visible theme, what lies beneath it is a rich, complex and thoroughly satisfying examination of life" (51). These reviewers have appreciated the ways Piercy has written of and used language that evokes the messiness and sensuousness of bodies and of lives.

In his review of *Braided Lives* for the *Times Literary Supplement,* Roger Seruton found nothing positive to say about the novel. He described the book as "written in a chatty, cluttered style," composed of a "succession of mundane episodes"; and, he associated it with other "gynaecological novel[s]" where "the biological facts of womanhood pervades its pages and the reader is constantly assailed by gynaecological technicalities" (807). In a prefiguration of Seruton's review, Piercy included a review of a volume of Jill's poetry in this novel. In it, the reviewer, Sydney Craw, writes: "In art there can be no special pleading for women. Her poetry is uterine and devoid of thrust. Her volume is wet, menstruates and carries a purse in which it can't find anything" (500). Piercy's work explores the inability of the literary establishment to appreciate writing about the realities of women's lives, something that seems especially undervalued by male critics; women reviewers, while still critical, seem to better understand the importance of the experiences Piercy has chosen to write about. Kerstin Shands described *Braided Lives* as "a passionate plea for women to control their own lives and their own sexuality" (105).

Braided Lives and *Small Changes* wrestle with similar topics, leading Shands to observe that in these two novels, "more clearly than other novels by Piercy," Piercy "describes and analyzes gender roles and relations, vividly reflecting women's, and in some cases, men's increased awareness and change, . . . the slow exodus out of patriarchy" (43). In *Small Changes,* Piercy gestured to an enlarged notion of what societal changes might be made. Elaine Tuttle Hansen said of this novel, "whether it succeeds or fails in the attempt to set new standards and say new things, it raises questions that are on the cutting edge of feminist aesthetics and feminist theory, and it repays critical analysis."

Small Changes traces the different paths of development and growth of two protagonists, here Miriam and Beth. In alternating sections—"The Book of Beth," "The Book of Miriam," and finally "Both in Turn," we learn their stories. The novel opens with Beth's marriage to Jim, her high school sweetheart, which she soon finds unsatisfying and stultifying. Beth leaves, running away to Boston. When she gets a clerical job at MIT, she meets Miriam, one of the computer scientists, and they become friends. Miriam moves on to a research job at Logical Systems Development. When Jim hires a detective to get Beth back, she is forced to return briefly to Syracuse, but she flees again. After her circuitous return to Boston, Miriam is able to get her a job at Logical and Beth is able to arrange a divorce.

In the early days of Beth's marriage to Jim, she is unhappy and finds herself daydreaming the time away to dull the discontent. One day she resists that coping mechanism and discovers that "by refusing to let herself dream away that Sunday she remained conscious of it" (37). This forces her to acknowledge her own misery, suggesting that the first step toward being able to enact change is to be aware of the restrictive conditions of one's life and the impact they have.

As in *Braided Lives,* women accommodate men. Beth initially adapts herself to Jim, "learning him, trying to please him" (30). The societal expectations of what a woman should be are held against her. When they have sex, Jim is not concerned with her pleasure. When Beth bravely shares that she is not sexually satisfied by missionary position intercourse, Jim issues a command: "You better start shaping up as a woman!" (30), echoing the Freudian belief that vaginal orgasms are what determine a "real woman." Then, "Jim stayed mad at her until she began making noises like the movie actresses did" (31), successfully bullying her into performing to meet his expectations regardless of her own feelings. Beth felt as though "he was expanding and she was contracting" (33). When she escapes Jim and her marriage and begins to rebuild her life in in Boston, Beth starts dating Tom Ryan. He soon assumes they'll live together and when Beth refuses, he too invokes the language of psychoanalysis as a way to pressure her into doing what he wants: "I guess you're scared to be a real woman with me" (80). Carol Anne Douglas observed that "some male critics have complained that the men in the book are too obnoxious to be believable; few women will find anything unbelievable about them" (12).

Beth begins trying new things, evaluating what she actually and authentically likes and dislikes, buying books, sitting in on classes—all in an effort to educate herself about who she is and what she wants, and to resist the societal indoctrination and gender norms that have been imposed upon her (*Small Changes* 48–49).

Early on, Miriam is more sure of herself than Beth; she has a career and is more confident and vibrant, a more definite presence. She finds her early relationship with Phil vastly satisfying, but ends up in serial rotating relationships with him and his friend Jackson, to whom she is also drawn. The first time

Miriam and Jackson live together, she is enthralled by him in an all-consuming and somewhat unbalanced way. She recalls that this is "what she had always been told would be the true center of her being, the central act of her life. A woman loving a man." She has become "a loving," no longer entirely her own person (194). Eventually the three of them decide to live together. When that arrangement implodes, primarily due to jealousy and competition between Phil and Jackson; but, as well, because Jackson is unwilling to open up to Miriam emotionally, Miriam moves out and moves into a group home with some friends. She has decided that "she was terribly self-destructive and needed help" (324), and enters analysis. She begins dating her boss, Neil Stone, and soon marries him. Once she marries, however, Miriam melts into the societally-defined role of woman/wife: the nurturer, caretaker, domestic goddess. Initially she even welcomes this change, crowing that "I feel good as a woman now—Neil's done that for me" (330). Neil succeeds in his function as gender role enforcer, effectively controlling Miriam by insisting that she "act like my wife . . . act like a woman" (389). As long Miriam meets his expectations, which Neil never questions as he seems to feel "through and through that what he liked must be right" (470), she can protect herself from the "central terror of her life . . . that Neil would stop loving her" (461). Miriam finds herself resentfully aware that "Neil had become a subject she studied" and equally aware that "he didn't spend that effort studying her" (468). This is almost the reverse of Beth's transformation. At the beginning of the novel Beth is pressured into the woman/wife role, but she rebels and resists her effacement. She intentionally excavates her identity, step by conscious step. Shands notes that in *Small Changes,* "women's views of men undergo profound changes as they begin to locate their own perspectives and find their own voices" (62).

These plot developments allow Piercy to call attention to the distinction between therapy and consciousness-raising. Consciousness-raising emerged from the radical arm of U.S. second-wave feminism as a method of identifying inequality and educating for a politicized awareness. Carol Hanisch articulated the difference between consciousness-raising and therapy: "Therapy assumes that someone is sick and that there is a cure" ("The Personal Is Political"). Consciousness-raising, instead, helps uncover and demystify the realities of being a woman in contemporary society. The phrase "the personal is political" grew out of the women's liberation movement and was an acknowledgment that the events and patterns in women's lives are often similar. Further, these experiences are both impacted by political systems and decisions and, themselves, have political implications. Hanisch noted that through consciousness-raising, women come to understand that "personal problems are political problems."[5] Through focused small-group discussions, women would share their personal experiences. An understanding of the commonality of their experiences and causes of oppression emerges from these discussions, and women would be galvanized into political action, into protest, into action for change. Beth's personal growth comes, in part, through her participation in the consciousness-raising process.

In contrast, Miriam is convinced by her husband and her therapist that most of what is unique and special about her is wrong (359), affirming Hanisch's description of therapy. Beth tries to explain to Miriam the benefits of consciousness-raising: "You think it's your problem, your fault. You still see it as private. If you were in a group with other women, you'd find out that what you think of as your private problems are common" (515). It is much later in her marriage that Miriam realizes the damage done to her by therapy. When Neil asks when she plans to see her therapist Dr. Bachman again, Miriam recognizes his motivation, pointing out that Neil thinks if she has any criticism of his actions, she "must be sick in the head" (533). She refuses to go back to the psychoanalyst, saying to Neil: "He's your policeman. He did a job on me once" (533).

In Meryl Altman's article "Beyond Trashiness: The Sexual Language of 1970s Feminist Fiction," Altman noted that a frequent theme in feminist novels of the time was "a recurrent and devastating critique of psychoanalysis, and of the would-be normalizing effect of the traditional family" (12). Phyllis Chesler's study *Women and Madness* (1972) provided some of the sociological and theoretical material from which feminist novelists drew, as she described the gendered practices of the disciplines of psychology and psychiatry and exposed the impact of their pathologizing of women's behavior.

Miriam recognizes gender inequity from the very beginning of the novel, but not as a systemic, structural system of oppression. She can only see it in terms of individualized sexist behavior. Somewhat surprisingly, given her professional success and seeming sense of sureness about herself, Miriam is stuck in a belief system and a set of assumptions mandated by society: she needs a man for validation. For Miriam, a person must have a partner, and since she cannot envision a sexual relationship with a woman, she must have a man. Interestingly, although for most of the novel Miriam is more outwardly demonstrative and affectionate, Beth has a more nuanced sense of relationships. Even when Beth does not have a primary sexual relationship, she develops and maintains many close friendships. Once she enters into a committed sexual relationship with Wanda, the leader of her women's theater troupe, Beth continues to connect through friendships, primarily with other women.

Piercy noted that she created this novel as "the equivalent of a full experience in a consciousness-raising session for many women who would never go through that experience" ("Mirror Images" 214–15). That intent is exceedingly clear in chapter 5, which is written in dialogue and which mimics an actual consciousness-raising session. The issues that Miriam, Beth, and Dorine discuss stem from the same questions used to focus discussion in many actual consciousness-raising groups: What was it like growing up in your family? How do you feel about your body? What is your image of yourself and what influences your self-image? How do you feel and express anger? "Why do we hate ourselves so much?" (85–89).

One result of these sessions is that Miriam recognizes the need for other women in her life: "she felt a sharp need for women she could talk to about her life . . . [which] gave her a frame of reference drawn from other women's experiences" (256). As she comes to value this different way of making sense of the world, Miriam begins to resist the attempts of the men in her life to label her as an exception, a pseudo-compliment they have used to control her. She has always valued being seen as different from other women. Now, she has begun to recognize that the way men treat women (herself and others) is an indicator of gender politics and power imbalances; being the token "not like other women" is no longer a positive label. She embraces membership in the community of "Women," welcoming that connection rather than rejecting it.

When Beth begins to attend a formal consciousness-raising group, she does not initially label it consciousness-raising but calls it "a group of women that meet together at M.I.T. and talk once a week" (249). It is only later that she is able to name the process as consciousness-raising; part of Beth's learning through this particular group enables her to recognize that the other women in the group are students who have "different problems than I do" (261). She is especially conscious of the students' lack of awareness of their own class privilege in comparison to her class status: "They have families taking care of them . . . and they'll have professions . . . They just plain can command more money" (261). The knowledge that Beth gains from consciousness-raising allows her to define some of her needs and to work to achieve them in her own life. She wants "to hold and be held, to feel myself doing good work, to feel myself with others that I love, to be able to say out loud what I think and feel" (504). She is not looking for material things, but for satisfying experiences and interpersonal relationships, for self-knowledge and psychic strength.

One early act of resistance Beth performs when she first arrives in Boston is writing her thoughts and inspiration on the walls of her small, shabby apartment. Having this private space, this room of her own, is important to Beth and also enables her creative expression—reminiscent of Piercy's own adolescent experience. She is actively claiming the right to have her own thoughts and to express them. One of Beth's statements is "LOVE IS WHAT WOMEN DO INSTEAD OF KNOWING OR FIGHTING OR MAKING OR INVENTING" (244). Here "love" is gendered and is not seen as a valued activity (by Beth or by society), as are all the other actions listed. Beth only begins to see loving as a positive action, as a rewarding choice, after her first sexual experiences with a woman. She observes the difference between being an actor in sex and being acted on; she sees what it means to "*make* love" (321). As Beth considers the functions that society associates with loving (for women), household maintenance surfaces as a major issue. Her description is passive; it is necessary for the "garbage to vanish" (244). This is how household maintenance appears to the people who do not have to do it (men, mostly), who do not have to be conscious of it being done, who do not have to accept responsibility for paying attention to it, who can simply assume that it is taken care of.

One of the achievements of the women's house Beth moves into is to acknowledge and actively engage with this issue. When the women divide up the household chores, they are aware of the costs, benefits, and energy expended in performing each one. It takes sustained work and conscious effort to have a fair system of household maintenance which appreciates the skills of each member and manages to get the drudgery done as well. As Piercy observes, "the novel is as much about who is doing the housework at any given point as it is about who is sleeping with whom" ("Mirror Images" 215). Negotiating and reconfiguring conventional domestic arrangements reflects activism that would challenge the structure of the patriarchal household and the limited roles it prescribes for women.

In addition to making the politics of domesticity visible, *Small Changes* presents a continuum of differing forms of public dissent. Phil marches in protests, gets clubbed, gassed, and so on. He supports war protestors who set off a bomb at Tech Square, which Beth thinks is pointless; she feels that the incident only served to make the Movement feel like they were doing something. Beth marches in a gay and lesbian pride parade reluctantly, not because she objects to the parade but because she feels it pushes her into making a public declaration about her sexuality that she is not yet convinced is true.

Beth is not averse to public political work, but she expresses her resistance in ways that she feels are more effective and authentic for her. Her consciousness-raising activities in the women's theater are an avenue through which to enact political beliefs. The collective, collaborative, and prefigurative theater activities are dissenting acts, not only in the content of any specific performance, but in the process of co-creating performances where power is shared and multiple voices are heard. So, consciousness-raising opens up a path into activism for Beth that is about imagining and creating new ways of living in relationship with people, as well as raising other women's consciousness through participatory theater.

Late in the novel, after Beth and Wanda have become lovers and partners, Wanda is forced to appear before a grand jury seeking information about her former husband, Joe, who, law enforcement believes, is assisting draft dodgers to flee to Canada. Although she is no longer emotionally or legally attached to Joe, Wanda refuses to cooperate with what she sees as a corrupt system: "they're my enemies much worse than he is" (491). This refusal to cooperate leads to a contempt charge and Wanda ends up serving time in a federal prison, relying on Beth to take care of her two children, Luis and Johnny. Instead, Wanda's parents petition for and successfully win custody of the children and they are taken from Beth. Because of Wanda's prison sentence and Beth and Wanda's lesbian relationship, their lawyer advises that they "haven't a chance of getting them back" (511).

Although Wanda had refused to run away with Beth and the children to avoid her incarceration, knowing that "we would have been hunted by the F.B.I." (510), she is clear that once she is released, she will get the children back with or without Beth. Wanda tries to impress upon Beth the difficulty of life as a fugitive, but Beth refuses to be left behind arguing that "we can't let them bust us up" (512). So, after Wanda is released, the two of them rescue her children, adopt false identities, and relocate. During a surreptitious stop at Miriam's house, Miriam is confused about how they can be happy while they are engaged in such risky behavior. Beth tells her that "we've been criminals since we began to love each other" (527). Wanda explains that freedom means not just her release from jail, but also their "freedom to act and fight" (527). Once Wanda, Beth, Luis, and Johnny are safe and living under fake names in another state, Beth joins another consciousness-raising group. At this point, she doesn't particularly feel a need to have her consciousness raised any further, but sees the group as a way to connect with other women and get involved in the local community. Here the consciousness-raising group is a mechanism for Beth to gain access to political activity and to build relationships; joining it is an intentional, planned strategy to enable action.

The novel foregrounds the need for new ways of being in relationship as it describes multiple options: Miriam, Phil, and Jackson experiment with group marriage for a time since Miriam loves them both and they both purport to love her; Dorine is tangentially included in this arrangement as an additional sexual outlet for Phil. The Going-to-the-Sun commune is less a consciously established commune than a group of people who happen to be inhabiting the same house—Miriam observes that it is "not a together commune" (214)—but it is shared living space that expands the notion of one-couple-per-household (213–19). Beth has a vision of making a home with other women where "we help each other sometimes, instead of always giving and giving and taking care of men and making them feel strong" (249). For a time Beth intentionally chooses celibacy and solitude, finding loneliness "a positive thing, a free space" (47). Beth later lives with the "women's theater house" (425), which is "not a close-knit family but tribal" (426). When she and Wanda and the children move to Cleveland under fake identities, they all want a different living arrangement. Cindy/Beth notes that "it's more work, just four of us" and Robert/Luis asks "how come at least we can't live in a commune?" (531) Piercy also presents the nuclear, traditional family through Miriam, Neil, and their two children, an arrangement which seems doomed to destroy either Miriam or itself (533–42).

Beth exhibits her understanding of the politics of relationship when she rejects the possibility of an ongoing liaison with Jackson. Throughout the novel, there is chemistry between them and they are intrigued by each other. After they finally have sex, Jackson challenges her to come and live with him, but Beth fires back: "I don't want to fight with you inside a household. I'd rather fight City Hall. I'd rather fight the system that made us both" (508). Although an important part of Beth's activism is about changing what it means to be "inside a household" for individuals, she also sees an extended impact beyond her own personal situation: "I want to love somebody and face outward and struggle to change things that hurt me and hurt others" (507). She wants a better society, a collective impact: "I can't define a victory that would be just for me . . . When we win . . . we'll all sit down at the table" (521–22). Beth understands the need for systemic change, seeing her life and work as part of the struggle to achieve that change for everyone. She has to come to awareness, to consciousness, in order to develop a strong sense of herself. She can then articulate what she wants in a relationship, work, and life, and be part of the effort to make those possibilities available to everyone.

The fight against systems of oppression as well as Beth and Wanda's decision to live as fugitives with Wanda's children foreshadows Piercy's 1979 novel *Vida*. The motivation for Beth and Wanda's flight is the fear of losing custody of Wanda's children; the couple is vulnerable because of their lesbianism and due to Wanda's stint in prison. In contrast, Vida is forced to live as a fugitive because of her political resistance and her work in several radical organizations, including the Movement, the Network, and the Little Red Wagon Collective. Although Beth and Wanda are able to settle down and build a new home in one place, albeit with pseudonyms and fake herstories, Vida is constantly on the move; constantly changing her appearance, name and back story; carrying most of what she still owns in her backpack; cautiously communicating and planning with her group, the Network. Piercy has commented that "*Vida's* still one of the most accurate portrayals of life underground, what led to it, and how the people survived" ("Living off the Grid" 55).

At the beginning of the novel, Vida is on her way to meet her husband, Leigh, whom she misses deeply and is able to see only rarely. During this trip, she learns that he has gone ahead with divorce proceedings because of pressure from his new girlfriend, Susannah. Before Vida fled underground, she and Leigh had an open marriage and both were and have continued to be involved with other lovers. Still, for Vida, her marriage and relationship with Leigh is one of her primary emotional anchors. Now he has been living with Susannah for several months, a situation which is clearly more serious than Vida anticipated or likes.

Leigh continues to work in New York City as a leftist radio personality doing a morning interview program and writing for various publications. He describes himself as "one of the most prominent media voices on the left" (44). He has been able to maintain a comfortable life, even as Vida was forced underground, because he reported on but was separate from most of the Movement's activities. This reunion comes at a new point of danger for Vida as one of their former Network members (and her former lover) Kevin has been apprehended by federal agents. Although a furious Kevin had left the group after being thrown off the board, and although Vida and Kevin are no longer connected, Vida notes that she is "scared when they catch anybody" (28); her reaction is similar to Wanda's when Wanda is called to testify for the grand jury. Whatever negative things have happened in interpersonal relationships, the apparatus of the state is the larger enemy.

Vida becomes even more concerned when she sees Lohania in one of the newspaper photographs with Kevin. Initially part of their core group, Lohania had been busted some years ago. After being "injured by drugs and prison," Lohania "could not quite be trusted" (107). The news coverage means that photos of Vida from years ago resurface in the paper, making her more identifiable. The actions of their small collective, the Little Red Wagon—consisting of Vida, Lohania, Kevin, Randy, and Jimmy (but not Leigh)—are rehashed in the media, along with other Network and Movement activities. In her conversation with Leigh, parts of their earlier history with the group arise, alluding to philosophical and ideological differences within radical movements. Kevin and Leigh had disagreed politically, as Kevin believed "in the need for armed struggle" (29), while Leigh did not. Kevin's arrest now makes the group and their past activities visible, and everyone is made more vulnerable.

During her trip across the country from her current hideout in L.A. to see Leigh and then to attend the annual Network board meeting, Vida stopped to check in with several of their members, but she had the sense that "the Network was drifting perilously" (41). Their fugitive status and their need to stay underground has come with a concomitant lack of access to public awareness and popular support. There are a few committed souls still involved, but they continue to be sought by the government and are at seemingly constant risk of arrest and jail. They are frustrated because despite all their work, sacrifice, passion, research, analysis, risks, strategies, and actions, they feel ineffective because the rich keep getting richer by exploiting both the poor and the environment. Marcie Hershman observed that "as Vida and the Network write position papers that they're not sure anyone will read, plan actions that are either ignored by the media or viewed as little more than outmoded pranks, as they rededicate themselves again and again to their concept of revolution, they're haunted by the fear: is anyone listening" (90). Vida's current research project is an analysis of international capital and what it might mean for the Left, but it's not enough. She wonders "what the hell was the Network doing with itself?" (77)—feeling that the "organization must act or rot" (189). If their ability to work towards their goals is circumscribed and stifled, how can they make societal change?

After her encounter with Leigh, Vida waits until it's safe to reconnect with her sister Natalie, who has a political job for her; Network colleagues arrange for a place for Vida to shelter safely in the meantime. Joel White, who she recognizes as a military deserter, is staying in the same safe house; he had been loosely connected to the Network but Vida had barely known him then. At first she is relieved: "he had been under a long time, and he was safe" (74). Later she becomes wary about his lack of constant vigilance and his impulsivity. Vida remembers "when half the police in the country seemed to have nothing to do but search for them . . . no time for laying down new lives, no time for anything but running" (165). Hyperawareness is what has kept her safe so far. As she says to Leigh, "habit saves. Or habit betrays" (208).

The novel bears witness to the historical moments of the counterculture, the anti-war movement, and the split between the New Left and the burgeoning women's movement. The primary narrative motivation for relating these histories is Joel's lack of knowledge. Shortly after he and Vida become lovers, Joel begins to complain: "You give me these glib answers. All these names. I'm supposed to be a newspaper morgue of old radical history. Either tell me the whole thing or tell me to shut up" (107). Piercy's readers may also be uninformed about these events, so this plot technique is useful to educate readers as well. As Vida tells Joel "the whole thing," the time frame of the novel vacillates from the past to the present. She is relating her own individual history, the history of her family, the history of her marriage—all inseparable from the political/social history of a part of her generation. Hershman noted that "by shifting back and forth between the two decades, Piercy is forcing us to view them not as separate chunks of time—hippie and antiwar versus Me and bourgeois temptation—but as part of a single historical flow" (90).

Various interpretations of what history is and what it does surface at another moment in the novel. Engaged in a conversation with Natalie and Lohania during one moment of their anti-war struggle, Vida describes feeling that there are pivotal moments in history and she is involved in one. "We're making history," she asserts proudly (125). Lohania's Marxist-inflected belief that "history is a science" then contradicts Natalie, who sees clearly that "history's a myth" (125). Natalie recognizes that although a basic fact or experience exists, the interpretation that is placed on it—even whether or not it is considered worthy of note and counts as part of history—is mediated by who becomes authorized to tell and validate that history.

Early on, they all belonged to Students Against the War (SAW). Despite differing political allegiances and ideologies, they were able to agree that "what mattered was the politics of the act" (126). Vida argues with Larkin, a Vietnam-vet amputee, because he wants to put all their effort into getting people out to a demonstration while she "wants the kids to learn how the power structure functions" (138). Larkin has a single focus: "All I care about is ending the war." Vida cares about and works toward that, too, but her plan is more long-term: "I also care about building a movement for social change that will survive the end of the war" (139). She wants more than one successful demonstration or action; she wants to build a sustained capacity to enact change.

Vida feels distant from Leigh as they prepare for a demonstration in which he will not be participating. He reports on the demonstration, which is "useful to all of them, the voice telling people not present what was going on; yet he faced little danger" (144); this detachment is what later enables him to continue to lead a fairly conventional life without concern of arrest and persecution. Vida notes the irony that his "work made him more respectable as he covered their work, which drove them farther and farther outside the hedges of legality" (247). At the demonstration, the need to attend to political education, as Vida had insisted, becomes clear when some of the demonstrators lose their focus on the target of the action—"the limousines" transporting powerbrokers attending a foreign policy meeting—and begin hassling "regular cars" (146). Vida helps redirect them, keeping all the demonstrators focused on the target of the protest.

Although Natalie and Vida are both involved with SAW and with the Movement, Vida is more active and in a more prominent leadership role. Natalie's bifurcated responsibilities move between the Movement and her marriage and children; and her politics begin to diverge, too, as Natalie gets more involved in women's issues which Vida at first sees as frivolous. Vida is focused only on the Movement and the Little Red Wagon Collective. She works "in the nerve centers of antiwar activity" (223). Even in a conversation with Natalie about rape,

Vida cannot quite understand why working on an issue like rape is important in comparison with the anti-war effort; she doesn't see it yet as political. Natalie is appalled, recognizing the substantive impact of gender-based violence: "Terror exercised by half the population over the other half isn't political?" (230). Ideological differences also impact Vida and Leigh's relationship. Vida notes, "right now we don't agree politically" (231), something that impedes her ability to feel close to her husband.

When, in the present, Vida is able to meet Natalie in Boston, introduce her to Joel, and find out the details of the job Natalie has arranged, she is surprised that Natalie is not shocked at her involvement with a younger man. Natalie observes that if women want equal relationships, "it's very young men or women, that's the only choice we all get now. The men our age won't change with us, won't let go of the old privileges . . . it's younger men with less stakes in the old roles, or women" (158). Natalie is now working at a battered women's shelter where a client—whose husband is a cop—and her children need to be transported to safety in New England. This is also good for Vida since it puts her geographically closer to where she needs to be for her next meeting with Leigh, and to reconnect with the Network board. Joel is pleased because the job provides a way to earn money; he is not yet in Vida's confidence about the Network and is unaware of both the upcoming board meeting and her planned rendezvous with Leigh. After many tense incidents—including the woman's reluctance to pay them the first half of the fee, uncooperative children, and a snowstorm—they are able to move her and her children successfully to the next stop in their escape. It's a task that, earlier on, Vida might not have recognized as political. Now she can see the connections between the power and control exerted in domestic violence and the power and control structuring society at large.

The constant absence of contact with family is painful for Vida. She cannot be honest with her mother Ruby, about where she is or what she is doing, or even talk to her directly very often; she cannot call Natalie or Leigh when she wants, but only in accordance with a pre-arranged, coded schedule. She has to live always on edge, always watching, never trusting anyone. She cannot earn money at a legitimate job, which forces her to rely on others for food, housing, money, and information—all things that makes her vulnerable. When she meets Leigh briefly in Vermont on the way to the Network meeting, she learns that Ruby has had a heart attack and is in the hospital. Vida feels helpless, but there is nothing she can do until she learns more from Natalie. Leigh also tells her that he thinks Kevin is talking to the authorities, since some of the charges against Kevin have been dropped and he is out on bail, most likely as part of a plea deal.

As the novel shifts back to 1970, the Little Red Wagon Collective gets blueprints through Randy for the Rockefeller Center recruitment office and the Whitehall Induction Center; he is also going to provide dynamite for a bomb. Although Randy's access to information and materials is convenient to enable action, it becomes problematic. As they're debating which location to hit, they learn that the National Guard has killed protesters at Kent State. This outrages and galvanizes the Little Red Wagon and also prompts a meeting of the SAW Steering Committee. SAW quickly organizes a demonstration in which everyone except Randy participates. The Little Red Wagon chooses their target and decides to plant the bomb at the office at Rockefeller Center.

When Vida, Kevin and Jimmy are on their way to plant it, Vida realizes they're being tailed. After they are able to break free, she calls the apartment to warn Randy and Lohania. Leigh tells her that Randy answered the ringing phone and told everyone that it was Vida calling to tell them to wait. When Vida hears cops raiding the apartment, she immediately suspects that Randy is an agent and that he has betrayed them. (This turns out to be accurate.) Vida, Kevin, and Jimmy decide to find a new target and plant the bomb anyway since "they can send us up for twenty years on conspiracy, even if we never set off this damned thing" (263). They target Mobil Oil, mailing communiques to the press and setting the bomb to go off at night to reduce any risk of casualties. This begins their time on the run as fugitives engaging in other political actions, eventually building the Network with other allies and colleagues.

After being on the run for a year or more, they take refuge at Hardscrabble Hill, an isolated farmhouse sheltering several other Network people. Vida and Kevin, who have been intimately involved, are at odds with each other and estranged, although they are still on the Network central committee along with Roger, Kiley, and Lark. During a visit by Lark, things between Vida and Kevin escalate when he breaks into her room and threatens her physically, something completely unacceptable to her and the others. Lark intervenes and takes Vida to New York to help deal with Network business. Seeing an end to the war, the Network decides to broaden its target areas, determining "to work more on our mass politics" (358) and to establish a new agenda and set of priorities, including connecting to liberation struggles abroad, and building relationships in the U.S. to women's liberation, labor rights, and gay liberation. At the next board meeting, Kevin is voted off the board and replaced by Eva, another fugitive and Network member. Furious at his ouster, Kevin leaves Hardscrabble Hill, recruiting several others to go with him.

Back in the present, Vida, Kiley, Lark, and Joel meet before the Network board meeting to plan their strategy, an awkward situation since Joel is not part of the leadership team and, before becoming involved with Vida, had been

Kiley's lover. The conversation immediately devolves into an argument about how to communicate with the masses. Kiley wants to publish a long position paper but Vida argues for communication without jargon, in a language accessible to more people, so they will understand the political stakes. To refocus their energies, Vida suggests a small, non-violent, anti-nuke action, thinking "we're old soldiers who feel better about ourselves when we're fighting" (278). The action, dropping balloons with warnings about the consequences of nuclear contamination should there be an accident at the nearby nuclear plant, is accomplished successfully. Then she and Joel head to Chicago where Ruby has had another heart attack.

Vida learns that Natalie is being followed in New York and also in Chicago at the hospital, with no care taken to hide the surveillance. Natalie says "it isn't to learn anything, because they're doing it openly. They stand outside staring at the house" (300). Agents have also interviewed Natalie's neighbors and subpoenaed her phone records. These intimidation tactics confuse Vida who "thought they'd cut back on chasing us" (301). When they learn that a grand jury has been impaneled in New York, Natalie becomes convinced that Kevin is talking. Although Leigh had also suspected this, Vida cannot believe Kevin would be so disloyal. In additional unwelcome news, Natalie also confirms that Leigh and Vida's divorce is final and that Leigh and Susannah have married. Vida surreptitiously approaches her brother, Paul, for help getting in to see Ruby in Chicago, and Paul tells her that Susannah is pregnant. Vida manages to sneak in to see Ruby disguised as Paul's adult daughter. When Natalie returns to New York, she is immediately subpoenaed by the grand jury. Concerned about what might happen to her, Natalie sends her kids back to Chicago.

On their way back east, Vida and Joel attempt to shelter with former Movement contacts in Cleveland. They have better luck with a Movement couple in Brooklyn where Vida falls ill, eventually recovering to learn that Natalie was offered immunity by the grand jury for her testimony. (Natalie refused to talk and she is now in jail.) Leigh misses his scheduled calls with Vida, who is forced to intercept him in public as he leaves work. In a conversation that quickly becomes contentious, Vida insists he continue to honor his financial obligations to her despite his new marriage, arguing that "new commitments do not cancel old commitments" (393). His life and freedom have not been compromised by the group's political actions; hers has. When Vida went underground, Leigh retained all their money and worldly goods; thus, he owes her financial support.

Vida reconnects with a former colleague, Oscar, who finds Vida and Joel a link to a possible job in Michigan in ten days, rescuing two kids who have been kidnapped by their father. The job will provide enough money to tide them over for a few months. Eva arranges to meet Vida and Joel before the board meeting and they connect at the home of Roger, another board member. Vida and Joel convince Eva and Roger of the value of proposing an anti-nuke action to the full board, and they find out that two more former Network members—Alice and Bill—have turned themselves in. At the board meeting they discover that the government is actively looking for Lark after learning more previously secret details about his identity. It becomes clear to everyone that Kevin and Lohania are indeed talking to the authorities, and after a heated discussion at the board meeting, the board agrees to an anti-nuke action, first at a construction site where a nuclear plant is under construction and then at the electric company's corporate offices.

Vida and Joel successfully prepare and set the first bomb, planted carefully to damage only equipment. As Joel and Vida prepare to go to Michigan to complete their job, they first must take care of a number of tasks in New York. Joel goes to collect the first payment of their fee and Vida is able to see Natalie, who has been released from jail. Natalie has to tell her that Ruby has died and that even Ruby's funeral was under surveillance, "swarming with FBI and red squad" (448). On her final errand to see their doctor, a Network ally, to refill prescription medications, Vida sees a news article announcing that Kevin has been shot and killed. He had been released on bail and engaged in a shoot-out with police; Lohania has been arrested for helping him. Kevin's cooperation with the authorities has endangered the Network but he did not completely betray his principles.

When Joel misses their planned rendezvous, Vida learns from Oscar that he is planning to crash a meeting he mistakenly thinks she is having with Leigh. She goes to the meeting place to intercept him, only to find it under surveillance. Leigh and Joel have both been taken into custody. Joel's inability to maintain discipline, learn from her caution and vigilance, and respect her experience has, in fact, compromised him. Vida thinks "because he had been underground all his adult life, it was too normal to him and he did not take the precautions she lived by" (477). Her instincts and caution, on the other hand, have saved her from capture and lead her to quickly alter her appearance and leave the area. After a few moments of complete distress—but not panic—Vida recovers and heads back to Vermont, reassuring herself that "she still had Natalie. Herself. Eva. Work. Her history, her political intent, her ability to cause trouble" (476).

Mary Biggs noted that Piercy's novel "works well on two levels: as suspenseful and deeply moving fiction, and as illuminating political and social history" ("Mixed" 226). Indeed, it is a compelling story, and the retelling of history is also important. The consequences of not having a full and accurate picture of the major social movements of the 1960s and 70s leave us subject to the limitations of mass media portrayals. Piercy's Vida finds that "years of reading her exploits in the papers had made her aware the newspapers were slightly less reliable than Marvel Comix" (165).

Much of what many of us "know" about the 1960s is limited to Woodstock and the lifestyle of flower children: hippies smoking pot, and a relaxing of sexual inhibitions and restrictions. The political analysis that drove one arm of radical protest and the deep desire to find new ways to live and to be in the world—that has been ignored or minimized in mainstream accounts. Vida speaks of "one of the best legacies they carried on from the '60s" which is "the wine-tart pleasure of believing you could act and change things and going ahead" (281). This too is lost in the popular versions of the times—the sense of possibility that the status quo is not fixed and that one can change things, and that there is joy and satisfaction inherent in that attempt. It is this less widely-known, less visible history that Piercy's novel recounts, reminding us that society and its structures can be remade and that we can be part of that effort. This continues to be the force that motivates Vida, even at the end of the novel when Joel has been captured: "I am at the mercy of history . . . but I can push it too a bit. . . . .Two steps forward and a step and half back. I will waste none of my life" (477). Vida retains the ongoing belief that we can—and must—choose to act. This is a poignant reminder that we each have some power in our lives, and that we should harness that power for positive and progressive social change.

In a post on her blog, Jo Walton observed that "*Vida* is a rare example of a mainstream book that is directly about trying to change society." However, the literary merits of the book exceed any strictly utilitarian or political purpose. Jennifer Uglow asserted that "the real strength of the book lies not in its historical analysis but in the power with which the loneliness and desolation of the central characters are portrayed." Romanticizing the fugitive life is not part of this novel. Uglow went on to insist that "it deserves attention . . . as a powerful novel, written with insight, wit and remorseless energy" (258). Elinor Langer also argued for the artistic value of the novel, commenting that "it is . . . a fully controlled, tightly structured dramatic narrative of such artful intensity that it leads the reader on at almost every page."

Piercy has punctured the underlying artificial and false dichotomy between political accomplishment and art: "The notion that politics have nothing to do with art is a very modern heresy. . . . For most of the world's history, poets have thought of themselves as human beings in a social web, with the same duties in the public sphere as anyone else, with the same set of human interests. My art is political, but no more political than a lot of art not so labeled, which also contains strong notions about what's immoral, moral, what's good and bad, having and getting, who's smart and who's stupid" (Betsky). Piercy's explanation highlights how the label "political" is selectively applied to literature to intentionally minimize and discredit artistic accomplishment. Literature doesn't change oppressive structures, but it can provide knowledge and vision. The characters in Piercy's novels are clear about what needs to change.

CHAPTER 3

New Histories

Gone to Soldiers and *Sex Wars*

Although all of Piercy's novels are rooted in specific socio-historical contexts, *Gone to Soldiers* and *Sex Wars* are two of the most obviously historical, deeply steeped in real people and places. Piercy's retellings offer new perspectives on pivotal historical events. The question Piercy has been "trying to answer in my historical novels" is: "how the hell did we get here?" ("The PEN Ten with Marge Piercy").

Gone to Soldiers and *Sex Wars* both reinscribe women and their contributions to histories that have otherwise been marginalized or made invisible. As Piercy has made clear in much of her writing, asserting women's presence and contributions in rich and robust ways is an important act. She also portrays women resisting and transcending conventional gender and sex roles and their efforts to build new kinds of intimate relationships. One experience common to both novels is that of women struggling to gain autonomy and assert their own voices, and to have those voices heard—Jacqueline insisting on learning to shoot firearms; Louise rejecting her role producing domestic war propaganda and insisting on telling the stories of women in the war; Susan and Elizabeth making a living on the lecture circuit; Victoria taking advantage of the latitude permitted to spiritualists to have a public persona—all of these are women insisting on the right to be their own person and to take their place in the world.

Piercy's World War II epic, *Gone to Soldiers* (compared by one reviewer to Don Passos's *U.S.A.*), gives voice to women's experiences of the war without negating the experiences of men. The six women and four men who live in the pages of this book directly challenge common wartime stereotypes; in particular, that of the gallant and heroic soldier off to fight overseas with his loyal and patriotic wife patiently waiting at home. Judith Wynn called the novel "Piercy's most gripping, ambitious work to date" and noted its impact as it "presents aspects of a World War II that are antithetical to late-show movie nostalgia." Andrea Freud Loewenstein agreed that *Gone to Soldiers* is "one of Piercy's best books" (26). Piercy's novel tells a wide-ranging story of World War II, in which the focus is not on leaders like Churchill, Roosevelt, Hitler, and de Gaulle, but on lesser-known historical characters and on a cast of fictional ones with narratives that Piercy signals early on will intersect and overlap. There is a romance-writer-turned-war-journalist; a white, Jewish, Chinese-speaking American who becomes an intelligence agent; a Parisian, Jewish teenager sent to live with relatives in the Midwest for her own safety; and more. Recurring themes throughout the novel include work, sexual coercion, and fluid family formation.

Piercy leads us to ask different questions about war than who won what battle, who died, or who sacrificed what. *Gone to Soldiers* illuminates how family and intimate relationships change in wartime; how power dynamics shift in multiple arenas in countries that are at war; and how resiliency is manifested and sustained. The book responds to Piercy's observation that "the roles of women in the resistance and the impact of the war on women and other civilians were relatively unexplored in fiction" (Weinbaum 102). The daily lives of Piercy's characters—including their loves, jobs, and need for diapers and food—are as important as the battlefield and war strategy. Her characters act occasionally as heroes, but far more often are simply heroic.

Mary Biggs found one trajectory of these stories—the shifting allegiances and love triangles of Louise, Oscar, Daniel, and Abra—less compelling than others, arguing that when contrasted with the reality of war, "the personal problems of American intellectuals seem frivolous" ("Fiction" 23). The activities of these characters may seem frivolous to Biggs, but this critique demonstrates a misunderstanding of the novel's effect. Part of the work of Piercy's novel is demonstrating how deeply and widely war impacts societies and citizens. Piercy consistently and emphatically refused to privilege one person's war experience or contribution over others. The lives of all the characters are deeply altered and often endangered by the war; and, their perspectives and reflections are important for understanding the significance of war in ways that include, but extend beyond, armies and battles.

Unlike many war novels, *Gone to Soldiers* has few battle scenes. The only traditional battle scenes in the novel are told from the perspective of Duvey, Ruthie's merchant marine brother, when his convoy to Malta is attacked (185); and Murray, Ruthie's fiancé, as he fights with his unit to hold Guadalcanal (214). It is a testament to Piercy's skill as a writer that she has so thoroughly put us in the heads of men under attack: their lives at risk, the incessant noise, the difficult physical conditions, and the nearby gruesome deaths of their comrades and friends. And it is part of the strength of this novel that Piercy has not valorized these moments in battle over other acts of bravery, other difficulties, or the more mundane activities that allow life to continue to exist. All the characters fight in whatever ways they can: Ruthie in the factory producing munitions for the war; Bernice delivering planes; Jacqueline in the French resistance and then in a concentration camp; Louise, first in the war propaganda machine and then as a war correspondent; Naomi trying to balance her existence in the United States with her knowledge of what her family is experiencing; and so on. Piercy has recognized the necessity of all of these efforts. As Freud Loewenstein noted, Piercy has written "of the 'ordinary' actually often courageous and extraordinary lives of working-class women" (26). Her confident and consistent insistence that the quotidian details of life are equally as important, significant, and worthy of attention as the decisions of politicians and generals, is characteristic of Piercy's work, and echoes the insistence of second-wave feminists that the "personal is the political" and vice versa.

One of the major strands of the novels focuses on the Lévy-Monot family, a French Jewish family comprised of Papa, Maman, Jacqueline/Yakova, the twins Naomi/Nadine and Rivka/Renée. Their story is told primarily through the perspectives of Jacqueline and Naomi. The majority of this novel is told in the third person, but Jacqueline's voice often comes directly through her diary entries which help us see her changing perspective as the events of the war proceed. Although their father is a Zionist who becomes active in the Resistance, Jacqueline early on claims to find no value in her Jewish identity: "as a religion, I find it absurd" (19). When France enters the war and the Germans arrive in Paris, Jacqueline initially anticipates and experiences little impact on her life, but the anti-Semitic messages and reactions she begins to encounter more frequently inspire her to assert her French identity: "I am as French as anybody else and as thoroughly imbued with French culture as any of my teachers" (21). When the family is forced to register and have their identity cards stamped to indicate they are Jews, and Jacqueline's dearest friend Marie Charlotte ends their friendship because Jacqueline is Jewish, she begins to understand that her life will not be the same: "Every day I feel less certain what is to become of us" (23). Whether Jacqueline identifies with her Jewish heritage and culture or not, it will have an undeniable impact on her life.

As the situation becomes more and more dire for Jews in France, Papa is able to sneak Naomi out of the country and send her to relatives in Detroit where, now called Naomi Siegal, she must pretend she has been adopted. Papa disappears on this trip and it is not until much later that Jaqueline learns that her father has been fighting with the maquis, small bands of resistance fighters living in the mountains. When Jacqueline joins the Resistance herself, she is unknowingly following in her father's footsteps. Later on in the war, it is their work as/in the Resistance that allows them to find each other again.

As circumstances become more difficult and dangerous in France, Jacqueline and the members of her family that remain are always hungry, always trying to obtain food; her gentile friends try to help by sharing extra food they have obtained on the black market. Access to food becomes a meaningful signifier of where one's political allegiances lie. Jacqueline notes that "you can tell someone's politics by their weight. That is, those who collaborate with the Germans are all plump and healthy-looking" (143). In addition to her appreciation for the extra food her new friends help her acquire, Jacqueline values their loyalty and the support those gifts of food symbolize. When the French Jews are forced to wear the yellow star, Jacqueline's non-Jewish friends wear one in protest as well (142),[1] thus demonstrating their solidarity in multiple ways.

As with many of Piercy's other novels, *Gone to Soldiers* makes evident the dangers of sex and the frequency with which women experience sexual coercion. Jacqueline's friend Henri, one of those helping provide food for her family, is attracted to her and becomes increasingly insistent that they have sex. After stalling for as long as she can, Jacqueline eventually acquiesces; but, not without weighing the consequences of refusal to her family's survival: "I like Henri a great deal, and without him and my other friends, we would be much hungrier" (145). Jacqueline is also curious, and she doesn't want to die in the war without experiencing sex, rationalizing, "I like Henri better than any man I have met, so why not him?" (145). For some time, Jacqueline's mother has been suspicious that Jacqueline has become involved in a sexual relationship with Henri, but the eventual confirmation of that physical relationship leads to a terrible fight, including physical violence, and a deep estrangement between Jacqueline and her mother. Jacqueline leaves her family home to stay with Henri in order to give her mother a couple of days to cool off. She plans to return to resolve the argument but she is given no chance to repair their relationship; two days later her mother and Rivka are taken away in a major arrest of French Jews, who are first confined in the Vel d'Hiv stadium. They are then moved to a camp at Drancy, and later moved further east to Dora/Nordhausen. It is initially not clear to Jacqueline and others what is happening at the camps. Months later Jacqueline hears of someone who "witnessed camps where Jews are sent" and claims that "most of the Jews sent east are not resettled but killed at once. The others are worked to death" (231). After their initial incarceration, we know of Maman and Rivka's experiences primarily through Naomi's nightmares, where she seems to be seeing through Rivka's eyes as Rivka and Maman endure the hardships of the camp.

As Rivka's twin, Naomi is tightly linked emotionally and intuitively to her twin's fate. As if through Rivka's eyes. Naomi sees the horrors of the camps, the filth, deprivation, and violence, and she feels her mother's and sister's situation in an embodied way. In her dreams, *"her throat was parched . . . they were hungry and thirsty" . . . "The hunger was the worst"* (166, 334). Naomi knows when her Maman dies (474) and, when Naomi stops dreaming through Rivka's eyes, she wonders if her twin is also dead (652).

Jacqueline and her dearest friend Daniela work with the Resistance. Jacqueline loves Daniela "as if she is my sister, my other self" (228), forging a new relational connection in the absence of her biological nuclear family. Working in a hospital—Jacqueline as a nurse's aide and Daniela as a nurse—enables them to make Jews seem to disappear by pretending they have died and then providing them false papers in a new name. Jacqueline is terrified for her mother and Rivka: "what saves me is the hard work we do daily in the hospital, and our lifesaving work afterwards" (234). This echoes a continuing theme in both Piercy's poetry and her novels: what is important is "to be of use" regardless, or perhaps in spite of, the personal trials and trauma one is experiencing.

After many in their Paris cell are apprehended, Jacqueline and Daniela are smuggled out of Paris to another active Resistance cell in Toulouse. The work to save other Jews is ongoing as Daniela continues producing counterfeit papers and Jacqueline travels with Jewish children across the mountains to smuggle them out of France. She is given the pseudonym Gingembre for her auburn hair and probably because of her sharp temper when she feels unfairly treated. Even as the Resistance cell fights against the German occupation, gendered assumptions about what jobs are appropriate for whom remain grounded in sexist attitudes. When the male leaders of the cell try to exclude Jacqueline from certain operations or activities because they are "too dangerous" for a woman (341), she refuses to allow it. They reluctantly acknowledge that Jacqueline is "quite tidy with explosives," but she notices that once the "plastique has been reduced by the touch of a woman . . . the men no longer compete to handle it" (480). The job has, effectively, been feminized and therefore is less desirable. Even in this group, where everyone is acting in solidarity against the Germans and the Vichy French collaborators and they are all constantly in danger, the gendered division of labor and other gender politics surface.

Although most of the chapters in *Gone to Soldiers* are told in the voice of or through the lens of one primary character, the chapter "One Cold Sunday" is an exception. This chapter includes reactions to the bombing of Pearl Harbor and the U.S. entry into war from a kaleidoscope of perspectives, including those of Bernice and her father; Daniel, Louise, and Oscar; and Ruthie, Naomi, and Murray. The narrative strategy Piercy employed in this chapter makes room for a range of reactions and emotions in response to the news and also subtly reinforces the value of multiple experiences.

In another aspect of the Lévy-Monot family's war experiences, Naomi's life in the United States gives us access to the stories of the Siegal family, particularly her cousin Ruthie and Ruthie's beau, Murray. Naomi is isolated from her family and country and is both scared and furious; she is angry with the "adults of the world, who seemed determined to ruin everything with their wars" and she is upset that this new war with Japan (after the bombing of Pearl Harbor) seems to be seen as a different war in the U.S. than the one in Europe that "her parents were caught in" (70). (Because the U.S. was bombed on its own soil, it seems to matter more to Americans.)

Naomi is terrified for her family and she feels alienated from the other children her age, for whom "war was something on the radio" (37), not something that impacts their lives the way it does hers. She becomes friends with Clotilde, a schoolmate from Martinique who speaks French and is also somewhat outside the concerns and interests of the other children, although for different reasons. Clotilde is Afro-Caribbean and racial politics impact their friendship, even though Naomi doesn't understand why "black and white girls were not supposed to be friends" (161). They keep their friendship a secret and talk to each other in French when no one else is around.

Ruthie is kind to Naomi, trying to help her improve her English and calming her nightmares. When Naomi gets her period, it is Ruthie she tells and Ruthie who helps and reassures her. Ruthie works full-time in a department store and goes to college at night, hoping to become a social worker. It is at school that she meets Murray and they begin a relationship. Ruthie and Murray both have aspirations and want more from their futures than they can see in their families. Murray's family was once middle-class; even though his father's car business ultimately closed, they remain tightly identified with their prior socio-economic status. The working-class position of Ruthie's family, despite her ambitions and drive for an education and Murray's love for her, does nothing to endear her to Murray's parents. They "had an idea of the girl Murray should bring home" (87) and it clearly was not her.

Once war has been declared, Murray decided to enlist in the Marines rather than wait to be drafted. He and Ruthie face the difficult decision of many young wartime couples: to marry before he leaves or to wait to marry until he comes home, if he does. Because of their dislike of Ruthie, his parents are worried that the couple might decide to marry precipitously. Murray, however, has a different perspective. Even though he wants to "demand that you become mine right now, before I leave," he also thinks it's not fair to marry Ruthie and then go off to war with no idea of what might happen (87). Ruthie promises to wait for him and they both concentrate on taking action to ensure their happiness and success after the war. When Murray comes home on leave, he gives Ruthie money to set up a savings account for them, which she knows "meant he was serious about their future" (207). During that visit, he also pressures Ruthie into having sex. She is initially both scared and resistant but, feeling "the slither of despair" (204) when he acts as though her refusal indicates a lack of real affection for and attachment to him, she ultimately agrees. Once she realizes "she was going to give in," (205), Ruthie creates a new interpretation for her actions, deciding that Murray "must carry off with him the knowledge of her love" (207) and asserting to herself that adding a sexual component to their relationship is a visible symbol of that love. Ruthie's retrospectively imposed romance is very different from Jacqueline's practical assessment of the benefits of consenting to Henri's desire for sex, but neither strategy dilutes the coercion employed by their men.

Ruthie becomes one of the women recruited into factory work to replace all the men who are away fighting. The factory jobs pay substantially better than any other job Ruthie has had, and she works the graveyard shift so that she can attend classes during the day. The sexual harassment is intense: "She was pinched, she was handled, she was stared at until she felt as if she were a mass of raw bloody tissue. She still could not cross the floor without forty men making lowing noises like besotted cattle or whistling" (197). The men resented the women, often sabotaging their work, worried that the men's own jobs were at stake. As more women joined the workforce, it got better. The "men could still be ugly but it wasn't full uproar when she had to cross the floor" (293). Later, when the war effort in Europe winds down, the women are targeted by mass media messages attempting to convince them that they "ought to all go back home and hang it up in the kitchen" (683). The 1981 documentary *The Life and Times of Rosie the Riveter* narrates this reality, showing examples of the propaganda pieces that enticed women into factory work by invoking themes of patriotism and support for the soldiers. After the war ends, the propaganda machine works in reverse, creating images of children being neglected because their mothers are at work, and displaying the gourmet dinners that women should now spend their time cooking. Eventually soldiers come home and the women are all laid off and disqualified from even entry-level jobs in the factories. Because of her college degree, Ruthie is somewhat insulated from unemployment; she is eventually able to find a position as a social worker.

As she grows into adolescence, Naomi also becomes vulnerable to sexual pressure and coercion. She can handle the boys her own age, but when her uncle Duvey is home on leave, he bribes Naomi to bring him his coffee in bed and kisses her each time. She doesn't quite know how to feel or what to do "because uncles had a right to kiss her, even if she did not want to, but not with the tongue" (256). One day Ruthie observes their exchange and then acts a buffer to protect Naomi from being alone with Duvey until he goes back to his ship. Even though Ruthie tells Naomi it's not her fault and that "Duvey was taking advantage of" her (256), Naomi has internalized shame. She feels responsible, as if she is the one who has done something wrong. When Duvey dies in his next Atlantic crossing after his convoy is attacked by German submarines, Ruthie cannot reconcile her feelings at his death; she tries to mourn for her brother, but also has "not forgiven him for tampering with Naomi" (291).

Naomi is later targeted and seduced by another adult male when Ruthie's high-school boyfriend Leib, married to Ruthie's best friend, Trudi, is injured in the war and sent home. He, Trudi, and their baby son, David, move into the upstairs apartment of the Siegal's house. It seems a mutually beneficial solution: Leib and Trudi want to get out of Trudi's mother's overcrowded house, and Ruthie's sister-in-law and her kids cannot continue to afford to pay rent on the upstairs flat and plan to move downstairs into the main part of the house. Ruthie is far from pleased with the arrangement since, in addition to crowding and the lack of privacy, "she did not trust Leib" (529). Rightfully so, since he soon tries, unsuccessfully, to pressure her into having sex with him.

Naomi, on the other hand, has a crush on Leib and is proud because he talks to her and "chose her as his friend" (563). Leib recognizes her vulnerability and pushes her into increasing physical intimacy in a very calculating way. The first time he touches her, Naomi is frightened but compliant. Leib is triumphant and pleased, crowing that "I thought you'd do anything I wanted, but I wasn't sure" (567). Ruthie sees that Naomi has a strong case of hero worship for Leib. Ruthie is a little uneasy about their friendship, but "she did not really suspect Leib of anything concrete" (618). Leib convinces Naomi that he loves her and she is "going to grow into my woman" (567). Naomi believes she loves him as well. When Naomi's high school boyfriend Alvin gives her a piece of jewelry, Leib is suspicious of Alvin's motivations and, despite her protests and against her will, takes Naomi's virginity (or, more accurately, rapes her). He feels entitled, claiming that "I'd be a fool to delay longer, for some kid to pick the cherry I'm waiting for" (656). He insinuates that he has been patient and respectful, but Alvin's and Naomi's relationship has impelled him to act. Naomi quickly becomes pregnant and, as she did after Duvey's sexual coercion, blames and judges herself harshly for permitting Leib to have sex with her; she recognizes that she did not want to have sex, but cannot really conceptualize what happened as rape. At the end of the war, when she learns that her sister Jacqueline is alive and coming to Detroit to see her, she worries, feeling that Jacqueline will expect a sister who is "still French, still good, still virginal" (759), seeing those states of being as identical. As soon as they are alone, Naomi tells her sister, "You don't want me. I'm of a bad character. I am pregnant" (764). She is surprised when Jacqueline's reaction is mild and non-judgmental: "You have the baby or you don't have the baby." Jacqueline's experiences during the war make conventional, middle-class values and concerns about morality seem antiquated and irrelevant. Her only concerns are to figure out what Naomi wants to do about the baby, help her do it, and take Naomi back to Europe with her.

In another thread of the novel, Bernice Coates is the linchpin around which the Coates family revolves. Her father, Professor Coates, teaches at St. Thomas, a small college in New England. He prefers a life of predictability and routine. The death of their mother Viola when she and her brother Jeff were both children has constrained and limited Bernice's life. At eleven, "Bernice had begun keeping house in deep confusion, with an inner prayer that her loneliness and her burden would not be permanent" (38)—yet, so far, it has been. In a practice reminiscent of Beth in *Small Changes,* Bernice daydreams scenarios of adventure and intrigue to escape the humdrum routines and responsibilities of her life. She earns some money typing papers for other faculty members, which she spends to buy an interest in a plane, hoping to log enough flying hours to earn a commercial pilot's license. Jeff becomes an artist and escapes the stultifying atmosphere of home by wandering around the country painting and working odd jobs to survive.

During their teenage years, she and Jeff become friends with a St. Thomas student, Zach Taylor, who Jeff has saved by pulling him out of the wreckage after a car accident; throughout the novel their lives continue to intertwine with his. Bernice has an unrequited crush on Zach. Zach, who comes from a very wealthy family, is a pilot; he pays for both Jeff and Bernice to learn to fly, although it is Bernice who most values this gift. She feels happy and most herself in the air. After Pearl Harbor and the declaration of war, Bernice volunteers for the Civil Air Patrol and "for three days every week she was ecstatic and useful, at one with the fabric body that extended her own" (97). Flying for the Civil Air Patrol allows Bernice to continue to log hours toward her commercial license and, she hopes, to eventually earn her instructor's license. Professor Coates is not particularly happy about her activities, since he is "cranky about his supper on those nights" (that she was flying), but "he could not fault her volunteering for the war effort" (97). Jeff, on the other hand, is commissioned as a second lieutenant in the Army and sent to Alabama as a rifle practice instructor where he is bored, miserable, and unable to find the energy and vision to paint. Bernice is frustrated because even if Jeff is not happy with his situation in Alabama, he is "fully involved" in the war effort; and she, too, wants "to take a real part" (100). She does not find her Civil Air Patrol to be sufficient as a meaningful contribution to the war effort.

In their youth, Jeff and Zach had briefly been lovers, and at Zach's instigation, Jeff is recruited to the Office of Strategic Services and trained in "guerilla warfare and in clandestine intelligence gathering" (136). Although Jeff is primarily heterosexual, he has had sex with other men "as a way of paying for a ride or a night's lodging" (138), which gave him insight into "a code he had learned that made sense of things that would otherwise have slid past him" (138). When Jeff successfully finishes his training, he is sent to London, where Zach—now a major—is also stationed. Jeff is given more training and occasionally assigned minor war-related tasks; being somewhat at loose ends, he begins to paint again. He finds his way into a circle of artists, where he meets a new lover, Mary Llewellyn. After Mary is killed in one of the London bombings when Jeff is on assignment in Algiers, he decides to transfer to Special Intelligence.

Jeff, under the code name Vendôme, is sent to support the Resistance cell in Toulouse. When he parachutes in with a cache of weapons and a radio operator to assist the cell's work, he breaks his ankle. After Daniela sets it, Jacqueline and Daniela are "delegated to see to his needs" (344). This infuriates Jacqueline—partly because she has "no particular talent for making chicken soup for clumsy American spies" (344) and she feels relegated to this caretaking role simply because she is a woman—but, more significantly, because he consistently and willfully violates their safety protocols and precautions. She is able to successfully leverage the duty that has been imposed on her, however, to force Lev, the cell's leader, to include her and Daniela in weapons training (something he initially refused to do because they are women). Jeff becomes attracted to Jacqueline, first because of her beauty and then because of her fierceness and courage. Although Jacqueline is initially immune to his interest, they eventually become lovers.

Their different histories and experiences during the war impact how they each see the world and any potential future. Jeff wants them to dream together about plans for after the war, which Jacqueline finds pointless. After what has happened to her family, her friends, and others, she "cannot believe in plans" (479)—she recognizes that "Jeff needs to dwell on a future in which we will be together," but she doesn't "believe in the world that much" (479). After they are captured by the Vichy French police when she and Jeff go to pick up information at a drop site, they are both tortured and Jacqueline is raped. Knowing they will be turned over to the Gestapo and acknowledging to himself that at some point he will "begin to say everything, everything, to stop the pain" (526), Jeff uses the cyanide pill he has been issued to prevent himself from betraying

Jacqueline and his comrades. Jacqueline escapes by discovering a loose window bar in her jail and works to create an opening large enough to flee. Later she learns that French construction workers made the "bar of freedom" whenever they could. They "would move one bar after it was inspected but before the cement hardened" (547), creating the possibility of escape. The determination to resist manifests in whatever small spaces and ways are available; there is always the possibility to fight back, to allow an intervention—however minor the opening seems.

Jacqueline flees to a mountain base where she finds her father, Daniela, and other colleagues, and she soon learns that Jeff is dead. Eventually she is given the information that he intentionally chose suicide to avoid betraying the resistance and finds that "I could not forgive him for choosing death" (551). Angry and deeply grief stricken, Jacqueline tries to comes to terms with his death and finds some solace in her "need to be useful" (552). As in Paris, being useful and productive provides her with some meaning in her life. When they stand guard together one night, Jacqueline's father shares with her his dream of reuniting their family and going to Jerusalem after the war to build a safe place for Jews to live. Jacqueline is skeptical that this fantasy is a real possibility but agrees that she "won't break up the family. I'll go with you" (578).

Jacqueline's diary entries end after their resistance base is attacked. Although a few remaining survivors of the Resistance cell are able to regroup, Jacqueline's father has been killed and she and Daniela are suspected dead as well. In reality, they have been taken to a concentration camp. Here we lose Jacqueline's first-person perspective, along with her diary, as her story begins to be narrated in the third-person. She has, Kerstin Shands noted, "become a nameless inmate in Auschwitz" (115). The conditions in the camp are as terrible as those Naomi has seen in her dreams. Starving; weak; subjected to frigid temperatures and random violence from the guards; and wondering "how long could they survive," Jacqueline nonetheless refuses to give up (629). She is determined to stay alive with her sense of self intact, whispering to Daniela and their new friend Rysia that, "I will not hate myself" because of how she looks and how she is treated and what she is made to do (631). She can resist mentally, if not physically.

At night she, Rysia, and Daniela dream about life after the war: clean clothes, good food, warm baths, and—Daniela insists—life in Israel. As the Allied forces draw nearer, the prisoners are taken from Auschwitz to the camp at Bergen-Belsen. Jacqueline watches for a way to escape. When the Allies close in and the SS marches them across the countryside, Daniela dies but Jacqueline and Rysia escape. Eventually they are found by American soldiers and taken to a hospital where they lose touch with each other.

Jacqueline's thoughts and attitudes progress from minimizing the harm of Nazi occupation to being outraged by its impact on her as an individual; from contempt for the violent arm of the resistance movement (in opposition to her initial non-violent practice) to acceptance of the need for a violent response in some situations; from a focus on survival (of body, soul, and self) in the concentration camp to her rescue and recovery in the hospital where Ari Katz, Daniela's former fiancé, finds her. The scars of war, of course, continue to shape her as "sometimes she found herself backed against the wall, trying to flatten herself out of existence. . . . She had been a piece too long, a slave, a number" (707). It is Ari who confirms that her mother is dead, Ari who finds her a job with the Americans, Ari who suggests they marry and go to Israel together. Jacqueline encounters Louise Kahan, who is able to locate a woman from the camps who confirms Rivka's death. Jacqueline finds and rescues Rysia from the streets and members of her former Resistance cell begin to appear. In an effort to recreate a circle of family, she determines to bring Naomi back from the U.S. and then to build a life with all of them. Jacqueline thinks: "The love she found in herself was not the love that Ari sought but deeper and more primitive, tribal, familial, sisterly, motherly. That she could give. That she would give. . . . They would cobble a family together out of refuse and rubble; they would scavenge their debris into a life" (751).

Knowing that Ari "needs someone to love" (766), Jacqueline "has already decided" that Naomi and Ari will marry (770). She plans to create a new model of family, built not exclusively on biological ties, but grounded in affection and respect for each other and in a shared commitment to the future. And she will do it in Israel, where she doesn't have to live among former French collaborators who adopted the anti-Semitic racism of the Germans.

Unlike her brother Jeff, Bernice's experiences during the war are stateside. Leveraging her work for the Civil Air Patrol, she successfully applies to the Women's Flying Training Detachment being organized by Jacqueline Cochran to ferry planes across the country. Her father attempts to forbid her to go, but she nevertheless reports for training in Texas where she learns to fly new types of planes and where she takes classes in all the skills she'll need as a transport pilot. She is embedded in a community of other women pilots and feels that she has "never been as happy in her life" (298). It is during her training that Bernice begins to wonder about what, in current terminology, might be called her gender identity and her sexuality: "She did not feel female; she did not feel male either, certainly not. What was she?" (300). She is still a virgin. However, all the other women have romantic histories or intimate connections with men so she "produced Zach" as the "man of interest in her life" in order to fit in (301).

When Zach, now a major, appears unexpectedly to take her out to dinner, he updates her about Jeff's activities and then insists on having sex with her. Bernice is clear that she does not want to have sex with Zach and tells him so. But, when he is clearly determined to proceed, she finds a positive way to frame his sexual violence, deciding that perhaps "this was the best way for her if she was ever to know what sex was" (361). She, like Jacqueline, is curious about what having sex will be like. Afterwards, she is a little surprised, and somewhat relieved, that "she could not identify in herself any different feeling toward Zach than she had before" (363). She has seen other women's lives change as the result of romantic relationships with men; it is not something she wants for herself.

As one of the Women Air Force Service Pilots, or WASPs, Bernice finds that at some air bases she is welcomed but, at others, the men "treated her as if she were a tramp" (353). Encountering uncharacteristic respect at one particular field, she soon realizes that "they had taken for her a man" (353); her flying gear has camouflaged her identity as a woman. Bernice's path also intersects briefly with Louise Kahan, who is assigned to a story about the female pilots. Louise is shocked at the sexist treatment of the female pilots and their difficult living conditions. For Bernice, none of that matters because "almost every day we fly." The message Bernice wants Louise to deliver in her article is that "we're good at what we do" (320). Because of this success, Bernice and some of the other women pilots are approved to ferry fighters across the country. Along with the women on the factory floor in Detroit, the female pilots face workplace discrimination and even danger. There are rumors that one female pilot crashed "from sugar in the gas tank put in by one of the men at that base who hated the WASPs" (443).

The women finally get uniforms, giving them more of a protective barrier and which signifies "one more step toward being a professional" (490). In addition to creating a more official status, Bernice finds that wearing the uniform "felt like a bit of disguise, cross dressing . . . a true woman would not be in uniform" (494). Here, again, Bernice seems to be questioning her sexual and gender identities in ways that overlap and are influenced by the gender barrier-breaking work in which she is involved.

Hostility toward the WASPs increases, particularly on base, where the men feel that the women pilots are taking jobs that rightfully belong to other men. Bernice and Flo, her closest friend among the other pilots, decide that after the war they'll go up to Alaska and see if they can make a career flying there. They begin to recognize an attraction to each other, "a wild surmise of something improbable" (586)—improbable enough that Bernice realizes her own ignorance: "to lust after another woman, she did not even know the name for that" (587). Bernice comes to realize that she is in love, "finally in love for the first time in my life, but with a woman. What will become of us?" (588). When Bernice receives a telegram notifying her of Jeff's death, she realizes even more intensely what Flo means to her. The loss of Jeff, until now "the only affection in her life," (638) makes her even more determined to find a way to be with Flo. Bernice is still unable to really understand how she might do that until a trip to New York. After delivering a plane, Bernice walks around Greenwich Village and finds a bar full of women. She allows herself to be picked up so she can "learn what she was and how to make love to Flo." She also learns that there is an identity associated with her feelings: "she was a lesbian" (641). This sexual experience and this label gives Bernice "permission to be what she was" (641), and helps her feel less isolated and alienated in her desire. There are other women who love women; she is not the only one.

Soon the pilots receive word that the WASP program is being deactivated. Despite their comprehensive training and best efforts, and similar to the treatment of the female factory workers who are fired from their jobs, few of the female pilots are able to find other aviation jobs. Luckily Bernice and Flo do find temporary jobs delivering surplus airplane trainers and, sharing a bedroom at a rooming house, consummate their relationship. Despite the dismantling of the WASP program, the male resentment of female pilots and the actions that endanger their lives don't stop. When Bernice is forced to land in the middle of one delivery due to weather conditions, she notices her plane is running hot and asks the mechanic to look at it. The next day when she is flying, her engine quits and she realizes he had not examined or repaired the plane. Bernice crashes. During her recovery in the hospital, she recommits to somehow make a life with Flo as "her wife" (646). After making a scouting visit to Alaska in male drag, she and Flo relocate to San Francisco and get subsistence jobs, finding their place in the local gay community. When they're hanging out at the gay bar, Bernice dresses "butch," feeling that she is "handsomer in male drag" (717). Her sense of her gender and her sexual identity has become more solidified, although her preference for male clothing doesn't mean she "felt like a man" (717). Her relationship with Flo makes her feel "more of a woman, not less" (717). Although she likes dressing as and passing for a man, and likes the benefits that attach to male identity, she is not confused or ambivalent about being a woman.

When Zach reappears and summons her for dinner, Bernice decides that he might be part of the solution to her dilemma. She thinks Zach might help her and Flo in their desire to build a new life. She determines to go see him "in full male drag" (721). Zach is startled but amused and sees immediately that Bernice has a plan and wants something from him. And, indeed, she does—a legitimate male identity with official papers and documents so she and Flo can go to Alaska and start an airline business, passing as a heterosexual couple. With her inheritance from Jeff and what she and Flo have saved, they have enough money, but Bernice needs to be able to appear to be a man to make it work. During the evening Zach offers some small corrections to "her performance" of masculinity (724), and soon he sends her a new identity as Harry Edward Munster (725).

The final web of relationships in this novel involves Louise Kahan, who writes romance novels under the pseudonym Annette Hollander Sinclair and socialist journalism under her own name; her ex-husband Oscar Kahan, a professor at Columbia; Oscar's research assistant, Abra Scott, who becomes his newest lover; and Daniel Balaban, a cryptoanalyst who becomes first Louise's lover and then Abra's lover and eventual husband. Their relationships and war jobs and duties overlap, serving to compete with and challenge conventional patterns of work and love.

Abra intuits that Oscar's research project with German immigrants has to do with more than its purported topic, the structures of political organizations. He recruits her to go to D.C. with him for a position with the Office of Strategic Services to continue doing what he acknowledges is intelligence work. Her cover is that she works for a government information office writing pamphlets. She becomes intrigued by the thought of Oscar as a lover and eventually seduces him. Oscar enthusiastically responds but lays out his requirements: "Abra, you want me, you've got me, but on my terms. We will play no games" (249). She agrees, finding "something had hooked her and hooked her hard" (250). It turns out that Oscar's terms include his being free to spend time with his ex-wife Louise, as well as other women with whom he has had relationships and require that Abra should exhibit "no possessiveness at all" (305). Abra finds it extremely challenging to adapt to an intimacy that is full of caring and passion, one where Oscar freely expresses his love for her, and yet be unable to have any expectations for or commitments to fidelity or a future together.

Daniel lives upstairs from Abra in D.C. and they become friendly through commiserating together about their relationships, both of them equally frustrated at their lack of control over those relationships. His cover is that of a government translator working with technical material in Japanese and Chinese; his work as a code-breaker is classified. Neither Daniel nor Abra are aware of what the other's actual work involves. When Abra and Oscar are transferred to London for a project, Abra becomes hopeful that away from Louise, their daughter, and the rest of Oscar's family, her relationship with him will grow into something more permanent. She finds some of their work in London "tedious and minute," but she is more disconcerted by the fact that some of their conclusions are not particularly welcome in London. Their analysis has found, for example, "that bombing was not nearly as effective as internal sabotage" (375), but the authorities appear unwilling to act on that information. Although it seems that the French Resistance has been more successful in opposing the Germans than some of the formal military groups, the resistance fighters are not esteemed by the Allies. Abra wonders if it's because of their politics—"the bulk of the Resistance was well left of center and a large and very active part of it was Communist" (376).

In the States, Louise begins to work with the Writer's War Board, helping to develop guidelines for magazine content and doing more writing about war issues, in addition to continuing to publish her romance novels. After her daughter Kay goes off to college, Louise decides to accept the Office of War Information's (OWI) efforts to recruit her to Washington where, because of the shortage of housing, she ends up rooming with Susannah, Abra's former roommate.

Although the government is encouraging women to enter factory work, mixed messages about working women continue to be disseminated. One of Louise's articles focuses on the children of working mothers; during her research she discovers that "all kinds of experts and officials are terrified because so many women are working" and notes the contradiction between that and the efforts to "recruit women into factories" (317). She also feels the campaign messages designed to "recruit more women into war work" are misguided. The data shows that women want to work for "economic motives" but the propaganda being created and dispersed is designed to "appeal to them as mothers, as wives," playing on their patriotism and asking them to show support for their men by joining the workforce (367). The idea of women's independence apparently continues to terrify; Louise's bosses will "only sell the war to women on terms that did not alarm men" (367).

Louise's move to Washington enables a friendship with Daniel, who acknowledges curiosity about her as he had been "Abra Scott's confidant" (369); Daniel initially knew of Louise only as Oscar's former wife. It is Louise who notices that Daniel's work doesn't seem to be what he has described it to be. She comments that "it's interesting how every time there's a major battle in the Pacific, you work round the clock" (371), an observation that surprises him in its accuracy. Daniel propositions her, discovering that he and Oscar "have absolutely the same taste in women" (371); Louise declines his advances, noting the difference in their ages as just one reason. Daniel persists, and eventually they do become lovers. Their connection is similar to Oscar's relationship with Abra as Louise loves Daniel but is not particularly invested in their relationship, reflecting to herself that she "would not be spending her life with him, so she did not feel deeply implicated in his habits, his decisions, his deep structures of belief or disbelief" (498). Daniel is much more attached to her. To his dismay, Louise accepts an assignment as a war correspondent and leaves Washington; she is relieved finally to be doing something that feels more useful. She also realizes that this is the first time "she had left a relationship while it was good, and for reasons that had nothing to do with the man's infidelity" (501), as was the case with her marriage. Louise is certain this means the end of their romantic relationship, but she cannot "sacrifice for a relationship she did not believe could endure long regardless" (501).

After a brief time in London reporting on the war and fending off Oscar's attempts to sleep with her, Louise is sent to the front in France, where she initially covers the medical corps. Conditions were hard, but she was managing to cope; and, "her adaptability shocked her" (589). A chance encounter with Claude, a former lover, gives her the chance to get into Paris ahead of the other correspondents; their driver is Ari, Daniela's fiancé. Since Ari is plugged into the Resistance, he is able to find them safe passage around the fighting, although they have to bicycle into the city for the last stretch. She borrows desk space at a clandestine newspaper and is there for the German's last attack on Paris; the clearing of the city by Resistance and French troops; and the German surrender.

When Abra learns that Louise is living in her old apartment and becoming friendly with Daniel, she feels "not only invaded but replaced" (379). Because intelligence from Germany is scarce, Abra and Oscar are helping prepare German exiles to infiltrate back into Germany to gather information. She writes to Daniel that, "I don't know what I might have done in this war more useful than what I am doing, but I doubt there would, honestly, be much" (571). After she, Oscar, and Louise share an awkward dinner, Abra begins to reconcile herself to the fact that although Oscar is "loving with her, he loved Louise" (606). Still, after Oscar is injured in a V-2 attack, when they are in the countryside preparing the exiles for their trip back, he suggests they consider marriage. Although she originally thought this was what she wanted, Abra has to acknowledge to herself to the fact that if, indeed, they marry, she will "always be the second wife, the imitation" (614). She wants Oscar, but she is strong and sensible enough to acknowledge that ultimately such a situation would be unacceptable to her. She begins to make herself "available" to other men, while still occasionally seeing Oscar (670), and then takes a new OSS job away from Oscar's unit in Frankfurt "studying the effect of the bombing on German morale" (674). This effectively ends her relationship with Oscar.

Daniel focuses on his work, decoding Japanese transmissions and trying to anticipate their military strategy. They discover that the secret weapon Japanese cables have mentioned are suicide bombers, the Kamikaze pilots. He continues to correspond with both Louise and Abra. With Louise, he feels he learns more about what she is doing from her war journalism than from her letters and, as the war ends, it is clear to him that their romantic relationship is over, a decision Louise had come to much earlier. As he and Abra continue to correspond, "he thought they had both come to appreciate having each other to confide in" (650). When Abra comes back to the States to decide whether to transfer to the Japanese bombing survey project, a project to which Daniel has already committed, they become lovers.

Louise goes to Berlin after it surrenders and covers the American discovery of the German treasure vaults, which includes items taken from concentration camp victims—wedding rings, dental fillings, etc. (688). Oscar shows up to inform her that his sister Gloria died in a concentration camp after she was discovered to be working with the Resistance; he continues to try to convince Louise that they belong back together. Louise "was not sure she was willing to be exactly together, but they did not seem any longer exactly apart" (693). When she collapses from dysentery and exhaustion, Oscar takes her to a rundown cottage in the country to convalesce until their transport home is ready to depart. Oscar continues to suggest that they become lovers again and reunite and, eventually, Louise agrees. As she remembers all the Jewish women who lost their lives during the war, she determines to "go make a home again and give thanks. Life is the first gift, love is the second, and understanding the third" (732). She is not naïve, however. "He would be more faithful than he had been," she thinks, but she is not convinced he will be entirely faithful. Still, "it would be the two of them alone together as it had not been for twenty years, and that would be in itself an adventure" (731). They are both different people and they will have a different kind of relationship.

Abra and Daniel marry and go to Tokyo to work on the bombing survey. Seeing the bomb site at Hiroshima shakes them both to the core. Abra reflects that she "married him because she loved him" but "now that they were together she was falling in love with him in a new way" (752). As Abra grows into herself as an independent woman, breaking her infatuation with Oscar and building her own life, she creates space for her and Daniel to build their relationship. She feels that they are "a team" (752) and "a relationship of equals" (753). She wonders, too, "having had this, what woman would settle for a rationed dependency?" (753). Both couples are embracing new ways of being together that differ from their relationships before and during the war.

The fluidity of movement in and out of relationships between these four characters is, perhaps, intensified by the context of the war. But, it is also because of the war that each of them has experiences, challenges, and opportunities that help them develop new attitudes about themselves, and toward relationships, finding new and more expansive ways to build intimacy, connection, and support.

Many of the women in this novel—Jacqueline, Ruthie, Naomi, Bernice—experience sexual coercion. Still, the end of the war brings with it the possibility of reconfiguring the gendered power dynamics that have been made conventional in intimate heterosexual relationships. Jacqueline rejects a romantic relationship with Ari, but will build a family with him and others. Bernice and Flo will perform a seemingly traditional heterosexual relationship in Alaska so they can be together as lesbians. Building on their history together, Louise and Oscar will resume their partnership, but it will have some marked differences that reflect their war experiences and the ways they have grown and changed. Abra and Daniel are creating a marriage that reflects reciprocity and interdependence. All of these situations represent hope: hope for peace, hope for happiness, hope for the future of the world, and hope for themselves.

Piercy has also challenged traditional configurations of intimate relationships and family dynamics in *Sex Wars,* here against the backdrop of the major political and societal changes underway in the late-nineteenth century. In her 2005 *Washington Post* review, Lauren Belfer remarked on Piercy's "gift for conjuring the texture of an historical era." In this novel, Piercy has retold the women's suffrage movement and its competing political strategies, a version of one-time presidential candidate Victoria Woodhull's rise to and fall from national prominence, the story of fictional Russian Jewish immigrant Freydeh Levin, and a recounting of Anthony Comstock's morality crusade. Unlike in *Gone to Soldiers,* where references to historical figures primarily serve to locate the action of the story, in *Sex Wars,* Woodhull, Comstock, Susan B. Anthony and Elizabeth Cady Stanton are much more fully realized characters and an integral part of the novel and its plot. In an interview with Heather Lee Schroeder, Piercy shared that the impetus for *Sex Wars* was "a longtime fascination with Elizabeth Cady Stanton," but that she could not find a way to write about her until she noticed that "there were an awful lot of parallels to the time right after the Civil War and the present. . . . The hot button issues of that time were censorship, pornography, abortion, contraception, the rights of women and minorities, immigration, the economy, should Christianity be the official religion, should the Bible be taught in schools and election fraud" (A9). Many of these major cultural issues under debate are highlighted in the novel, which also includes an exploration of the professionalization of medicine and its impact on women's reproductive choices, as well as the rise of spiritualism. In drawing from historical events for the plot, Piercy has made visible the untold stories—stories we do not learn from traditional historical accounts.

This novel is told entirely through the third-person perspective; however, the narrative lens of the chapters shifts so that events occur from the viewpoints of different characters. In fact, Carmel Morse noted the "rather unique narrative structure" Piercy has achieved as she "expertly weaves her diverse characters' lives together" (192). This technique also allows the reader to see the intersections, connections, and overlap between events and lives.

Victoria, her sister Tennie, and Freydeh are all struggling to achieve better lives, higher social status, and financial security and independence. As Donna Seaman observed, in this novel Piercy "portrays heroic women determined to control every aspect of their lives, from birth control to finances" (7). The characters show consistent and deep desires for autonomy, continually evaluating their situations and employing any advantage they have; they are all practical and realistic. Elizabeth and Susan are ensconced in a comfortable middle-class social status but still struggle to maintain financial security and to fund their activism. In their work to achieve political and legal rights, they are also strategic about leveraging assets other than financial ones. For example, Susan observes that Elizabeth's "authority as a respectable, married woman, mother of a tribe" with children is often a benefit that assures others of their respectability (32); Elizabeth's status as a mother and wife does provide, Elizabeth agrees, "a useful façade for a lifelong revolutionary" (33). They learn how important appearance is in order to be taken seriously. Elizabeth "had worn the bloomer costume for two years, but she found that no one could hear what she was saying for the commotion a woman wearing pants seemed to cause" (37). She chooses to return to more conventional dress so that her message can be heard more easily. Elizabeth and Victoria share the belief that "women had to be financially independent" (100); and, Freydeh also wants "to be independent" (30), to be able to make her own decisions and to have enough money to have choices. Elizabeth recognizes how unfair it is that women are paid less than men under the false assumption that their wages are "supplemental" when often the money they earn is crucial to family sustenance and survival. For Victoria, money "meant freedom, power" (102); the spirits have told her that she will "achieve wealth and great things" (107). All of these women are willing to dream and to dare to take risks in order to achieve their goals and dreams.

Victoria and her husband James are practitioners of free love, taking lovers as it suits them without any jeopardy to their own marriage. Victoria is very intentional and quite clear-headed in her selection of lovers and "was attracted not by flash or wealth or power, but by knowledge. Every lover was also her mentor, her educator" (170). She does not delude herself with fantasies of romance. Victoria has an unshakeable confidence in her own abilities:

"there was little of which she did not imagine herself capable . . . She felt she contained within herself a hundred vital magnificent women in potentiality" (51). As part of creating her future success, she plans to meet and learn from "artists, intellectuals, politicians, those who thought deeply, spoke well and made things happen" (53). Victoria strives to behave in a cultivated and sophisticated manner that masks her roots, but she wants to go beyond just performance; she wants the knowledge and information that will enable her to inhabit that persona in an authentic manner. She also has a clear understanding of the consequences of accepting society's judgments about women: "A so-called good woman often appeared a cipher, defined by what she wasn't and what she never had done and perhaps refused to let herself imagine ever doing" (50). Being defined by absence or limitation may be what society expects of many women, but this is not the kind of woman Victoria is or ever wants to be.

Victoria and Tennie come from poverty; their father has used them and other family members to run a number of schemes and cons across the country, including selling off Tennie's virginity multiple times and capitalizing on Victoria's talents as a spiritualist. Spiritualism has given Victoria access to a public voice since "women were not supposed to speak in public, but that taboo had been broken by women preachers, abolitionists and spiritualists" (108).[2] Now in New York, the sisters have a plan to cultivate wealthy businessman Cornelius Vanderbilt, using Victoria's connection with the spirit world and Tennie's gift for mesmeric healing to benefit from his patronage. As they begin to implement their plan, they make their living selling "medical items," including contraceptive devices, to brothels (6). During these sales calls, they develop friends and allies and garner information about the people and happenings of the city, all of which they put to good use.

One brothel owner in particular, Annie Wood, has become a friend. Her girls are encouraged to have their customers "chat about their business affairs and politics" (73), and then pass on any potentially useful details provided by their clients; some of that information has been useful in building Vanderbilt's trust in Victoria's messages from the spirits. In discussing investment strategies, Annie mentions that she buys land, following the lead of Madame Restell. Restell is an alias used by Ann Lohman, "the best abortionist in all of New York" (104), who has become extremely wealthy. Victoria marvels at Restell's success, particularly in the face of the American Medical Association's actions to make abortion illegal. But, as Restell later tells Freydeh, her services are necessary to many: "they scorn us, but they can't live without us" (185). Issues of access to contraception and reproductive control in the face of patriarchal attempts to restrict them are points of connection between these disparate women throughout the novel.

As Victoria and, especially, Tennie grow closer to Vanderbilt, Victoria begins to feel strongly that her desired success is "within her ken" (107). She shares with James one of her efforts: "I am trying to study rhetoric. The art of making speeches that actually move people" (109). Victoria wants to be influential. She feels certain that fame will follow wealth. Although Vanderbilt scoffs at politics, noting his ability to "buy and sell politicians by the carload" (102), Victoria and Tennie disguise themselves as young men to attend a rally in support of Ulysses S. Grant's presidential campaign because Victoria wants to analyze the speeches. As Victoria learns about "the political and intellectual life of New York" (169), she practices honing her public speaking skills, observing other speakers—including Elizabeth and Susan who are lecturing on the Lyceum circuit—in order to identify effective rhetorical strategies and gestures. She has become more convinced than ever that she has "a role to play in history" (170). At the same time, she is learning about finance and the stock market from Vanderbilt, because "the first step" to her goals is "still money" (170). Victoria strives to educate and improve herself so she is ready for whatever success she will find or create. Her determination and focus challenge stereotypical conceptions of the era about women's capabilities.

Freydeh came to the U.S. with her husband, Moishe, both in search of a better life. The noise of the city grates on Freydeh and, in a subtle commentary on the times, she describes what she hears: "always a murmur of voices, a huckster yelling, a beaten woman screaming, a gambler cursing, a mother calling out a window or up from the street" (115)—domestic violence is just one occurrence in a litany of other noises, unworthy of special notice. Widowed unexpectedly, she works in Yonkelman's pharmacy where all kinds of devices to "prevent conception or end it" are sold (18); Freydeh had decided that "making condoms was a great way to make a living," something she could do in her own kitchen and which would allow her more control over her life and her income (14). To that end, she takes advantage of a condom manufacturer's interest in her and, when he periodically visits the pharmacy to sell his wares, she engages him in conversation to gather information about the production process.

Freydeh receives a letter from her younger sister Shaineh conveying the news that their parents have died in a cholera epidemic. Shaineh is coming to New York by ship; she wanted "to go and be useful and have a good life there" (21). However, Freydeh doesn't receive the letter until months after Shaineh was scheduled to arrive in New York and is now frantic to discover if her sister indeed arrived and what has happened to her since. Her search for information about Shaineh and her attempts to locate Shaineh continue throughout the novel.

Freydeh has become friendly with Sammy, an abandoned street kid with better English skills than her own, and recruits him to help her start her condom business and to find Shaineh. After Freydeh rents an apartment, gets Yonkelman to hire Sammy as a delivery boy, and finds a boarder to share expenses, she and Sammy begin practicing and perfecting their production of condoms. The boarder feels this is "no trade for a respectable woman" (56), and she eventually moves out. Freydeh rejects the notion that working to perfect "a trade to support me" has any bearing on her decency and respectability, retorting that "this respectable woman wants some money" (56).

The concept of respectability is invoked many times throughout the novel: Elizabeth's intentional cultivation of the appearance of respectability in her dress and demeanor; and, Victoria's and Tennie's fervent desire to perform respectability appropriately so they can improve their class status. Historical and fictional characters reflect and challenge the restrictive notions of the Victorian moralist Anthony Comstock,[3] who labeled women either virtuous or amoral and sinful, according to his beliefs about what a respectable woman should do and how she should act.

The artificiality and contingent nature of the categories employed to police women's behavior arises while Susan and Elizabeth strategize and lobby in preparation for the upcoming American Equal Rights Convention. Theodore Tilton, one of their allies who is also an associate of Henry Ward Beecher, purports to share their commitment to the abolition of slavery and to women's rights. It is Tilton who initially proposes "combining the Anti-Slavery Society and the Women's Rights Organization into one organization," a strategy with which Elizabeth and Susan agree, believing that both groups were for universal suffrage and that "no group should gain equality at the expense of the other" (65). Tilton's interest in women's rights, however, does not seem to extend to his own wife, Lib; Elizabeth noted that he "treated his own wife like a wayward child," and that it doesn't seem like "Lib had been given much of a chance to develop her own ideas" (64). After dinner at the Tilton's home one evening, Theo shares with Elizabeth his discomfort with Lib's new expression of sexual feelings, finding it "unnatural" in a woman with "her inborn purity" (66). Elizabeth assures him that "women can enjoy the conjugal embrace as warmly as men," but finds it odd that Tilton, himself unfaithful, "should cringe at his own wife's ardor" (66). Victoria and Theo later become lovers, and she finds that he, echoing Comstock, "believed in good and bad women. The bad women were sexually responsive; the good women were cold" (291). Victoria does not agree with Theo, and she wishes to "educate him out of his nonsense about women" (291).

These varied notions about sexuality and morality, particularly in relation to women's sexuality, collide and compete throughout the novel. The availability of contraception; brothels and abortion; Victoria's advocacy and practice of free love; and Freydeh's identification of condom manufacturer as a possible career all belie the stereotypes of the Victorian era as one of joyless marital sex and rigid enforcement of female purity. But, these realities exist alongside Theo's negative reaction to his wife—a good woman—being interested in sex, as well as Anthony Comstock and his virulent crusade against what he determines to be immoral behavior and beliefs.

Calculating the possibility of success of their platform of universal suffrage at the convention, Elizabeth is counting on the support of Wendell Phillips. Phillips has been a long-time ally, and Elizabeth supported him for a leadership position in the organization. At the convention, however, Phillips, Frederick Douglass, and others change course to successfully argue to privilege the right "of the Negro" (67) to vote and to postpone efforts for women's suffrage until later. Furious, Elizabeth points out the irrationality of their argument: "Do you believe the African race is composed entirely of males?" (67). Elizabeth feels betrayed by Phillips's duplicity, which evokes the earlier betrayal of her husband at an Anti-Slavery Society conference in London when he voted against seating her and other women delegates.

Elizabeth and Susan respond by founding the National Woman Suffrage Association (NWSA), feeling that "we must build a movement of women, controlled by women, with women officers and a women's agenda" (69). This causes tension with other groups of women over strategies and desired approaches to change, which negatively impacts the NWSA's ability to build coalitions and raise funds. Some see their group as "too controversial" and "too radical" (95). Susan and Elizabeth are particularly interested in getting the support of the "Boston women" (95) for the NWSA, although Elizabeth finds the pretentions of those women and their attachment to the appearance of propriety a little hypocritical given that "their lives were not as conventional as they liked to pretend in public" (99). Many of these women were engaged in relationships "outside their marriages" (99); yet, they have money and "the respectability" which will help to forward the NWSA's efforts.[4]

In addition to recognizing the intersectionality of race and gender in the struggle for suffrage, class status is also relevant to and a determinant of women's experiences. Susan is trying to organize working women, women who do not have the economic means of the Boston ladies (95). In the speech Elizabeth writes for Susan to deliver, she points out that the alleged justification for women to be unfairly paid lower wages was that their income was "supplemental" (100), merely an extra boost and not a necessity in the family budget.

In reality, "often women were the heads of families, because of desertion and death or injury" (100); in fact, their monetary needs are no less than that of men. Elizabeth believes that "women had to be financially independent" (100), echoing the motivation that also drives Victoria and Freydeh.

As Elizabeth and Susan deal with the competition between their own National Woman Suffrage Association and the more conservative American Suffrage Association, they cultivate as an ally Isabella Beecher Hooker, a member of the prominent "Beecher clan" (98) that includes Harriet Beecher Stowe, author of *Uncle Tom's Cabin*. The American Suffrage Association is allied with the Republican Party and limits its focus to suffrage, appealing to professional and club women with the message that "suffrage is safe, you can be a lady and support suffrage" (204).

The compelling need to be seen as a respectable woman interferes with the organization's ability to work for women's progress on a wider scale. Elizabeth regrets the dispersal of energies and resources that results from having two organizations and "would have merged the groups if she could but not at the price of becoming respectable and banging away at one issue only" (204). She is determined to address "all the other problems and concerns of women" as well (204). She recognizes the connections between the many issues that constrain women's lives and the ways in which various aspects of women's identities (race, class, gender, and so on) interact to impact those experiences.

Elizabeth's understanding of complexity is not mirrored by Anthony Comstock's thoughts, practices, and beliefs. From the reader's earliest introduction to Anthony, he is self-righteous, rigid, and judgmental—certain that his understanding of what is moral and how one should conduct oneself is correct and one that others should emulate. He sees his role to convert others to his beliefs and to save them from their own wickedness. Anthony finds the availability of erotica, prostitution, and contraceptive devices deeply disturbing, as they provide opportunities for temptation in men and women less virtuous than himself. He is frustrated by his inability to take any effective action against this evil, until a leader at the YMCA draws Anthony's attention to recently passed legislation addressing "the trade in obscene materials" (82). After he assists the police in confiscating the materials for sale at one shop, he feels like "a light of rectitude and strength" (85). Eventually Anthony is rewarded in his efforts by being chosen to lead the YMCA Committee to Suppress Vice.

Anthony selects Margaret Hamilton to be his wife, a woman who seems to him to possess the virtues he desires in a wife: "a modest woman, a demure woman, a proper woman" (159). After recognizing he has no idea how to manage "marriage in the physical sense" (162), Anthony—in actions reeking of hypocrisy—visits one of the bookshops that carries the obscene merchandise to which he objects, buys sufficient materials to educate himself, and then brings the police in to confiscate the other materials in the bookshop. The first time he and Margaret have sex, he relies on his recollection of an image from the books he has deemed obscene in order to successfully maintain an erection and consummate his marriage. Anthony is very happy with his choice of Margaret, finding her "a neat clean obedient Christian wife" (204). As readers, we have no sense of Margaret as her own person; she is an example of the "cipher" that Victoria disdains (50). She appears only through Anthony's perspective and only in her designated role of "providing him with a home that was a haven from all the ugly things in the city" (250).

A third of the way through the novel, Piercy moved into the past, establishing the back story of her characters, including Freydeh's and Moishe's arrival in the U.S.; Moishe's death due to a freak accident and Freydeh's subsequent miscarriage; Stanton's entry into women's rights activism with the Seneca Falls Convention and the rift it creates in her marriage; Comstock's early infatuation with evangelical Christianity in its hellfire-and-brimstone mode; and Victoria's unhappy marriage to her first drunkard husband.

Returning to the present-day 1869, Freydeh's hours are reduced at the pharmacy, which impels her to act on her plan to move into the condom business, realizing that "she had to have the courage to do what she had imagined" (151). Although she is worried about financial security with a reduced paycheck, this decision also provides more flexibility for her and Sammy's time to search for Shaineh. As part of their attempt to find Shaineh, Freydeh and Sammy attend shul with some friends they have met, hoping to learn more about her whereabouts. Being more devout than Freydeh, Shaineh might have sought solace in the shul.

One of the men recalls giving Shaineh an address where she might find work as a seamstress. When Freydeh and Sammy visit, they learn that she had been fired for not being a fast enough worker and someone had sent her to a "madam that sometimes hires Jewish girls" (150). When they visit the madam, Mrs. Baines, they find that Shaineh had been working there, but in her misery from forced, commercial sexual activity combined with her fear of men, she had not been popular with the customers. Shaineh was ultimately sold to a client who wanted her. Baines's venality and lack of concern for Shaineh's fate is in clear contrast to that of Annie Woods, the brothel owner that Victoria has befriended. Woods wants her "girls . . . on the bright side" (73) and has them taught to read and write if they are illiterate. Her investment in her workers is good for business, attracting and retaining a wealthy clientele. Although Baines's brothel is "an ordinary respectable-looking brownstone house," she exhibits a level of callousness that belies her comfortable surroundings.

After some negotiation, Baines provides an address for the man who took Shaineh. The address is only a burned-out building, but this allows them to locate a neighborhood where they can continue to ask questions. Eventually they find Mrs. Connor, who saw Shaineh escape from the fire that destroyed the building. Connor also shares that a man kept her locked up and that she was pregnant.

Freydeh is sure that Shaineh cannot afford to have a baby and will probably try to "seek a remedy" (180). As Freydeh pursues every possible lead to find Shaineh, she encounters Kezia, another hungry and filthy street kid. Despite Sammy's initial objections, Freydeh welcomes Kezia into their home. As they socialize Kezia, they discover that she has artistic talent. She begins to draw pictures for the labels on the boxes of condoms, thus making them easier to market. Freydeh and Sammy get closer to locating Shaineh by identifying the man who had been keeping her.

Freydeh has also been sending money to her sister Sara so that Sara and her family can come to the U.S.; when they finally arrive, overwhelmed by the journey and the city, they are more than shocked once they enter Freydeh's apartment to find that she makes condoms for a living. All adapt quickly, except for Sara's husband, Asher, who thinks that the work is not "fitting for a woman" (315). His perfunctory attempts to find work are rarely successful, but he seems perfectly willing to be housed and fed with the profits from Freydeh's business, about which he maintains a judgmental and contemptuous attitude. In that sense, his mindset parallels that of Restell's clients: judgmental and scornful of her actions on the surface, but willing to benefit from the results of those actions.

The pace of the novel picks up noticeably as major societal and personal events begin to collide and the characters' lives intersect more often and more deeply. Morse observes that "Piercy packs a plethora of events, characters, and causes into this work of historical fiction, focusing on women's rights and gender roles that are in the process of flux and transformation as the novel progresses" (192). At times, the latter section of the novel provides more attention to recounting the parade of events that occur and gives less emphasis to the interior thoughts and feelings of the characters. Indeed, Belfer notes that "a profusion of historical detail eventually overwhelms the characters." Piercy's stylistic decisions do, however, mirror the sense of the time she is invoking; it is an era when much is changing, and changing rapidly.

Victoria makes a fortune in gold speculation with information she has gathered from Vanderbilt and others; she and Tennie start their own brokerage business as well as a publication, *Woodhull & Claflin's Weekly*. Victoria's alcoholic, drug-addicted first husband reappears and is absorbed into the household. She becomes active in women's rights and other progressive issues; successfully addresses a committee of Congress; allies with Susan B. Anthony, Elizabeth Cady Stanton, and Isabella Beecher Hooker; and decides to run for president.

Victoria's unashamed belief in and practice of free love is shocking to some of the women's rights activists, but Elizabeth supports Victoria's refusal to hide what she believes. Before Victoria's speech at the National Woman Suffrage Association meeting, Elizabeth responds to Lucretia Mott's objection by pointing out that "Victoria has the courage to say openly what people like Henry Ward Beecher and several of the Boston women practice secretly. Let us honor her honesty, Lucretia" (297). Victoria's speech advocating equality for women is well-received, but immediately eclipsed by a scandal in her family. Her parents try to blackmail Vanderbilt, and then her mother accuses Victoria's husband James of "alienating her children from her, for forcing them into prostitution and using them for blackmail" (297)—an accusation that is clearly false and, given the past practices of their father who prostituted Tennie, quite absurd.

The newspapers are eager to publicize the scandal, however; and, their coverage of Victoria changes as "from the bewitching broker and the female politician, she became the notorious Woodhull, free lover and communist" (298). Vanderbilt cuts them off, refusing to see or accept any correspondence from Victoria or Tennie. Theo Tilton, who has written Victoria's campaign biography and professed his love for her, betrays her by publicly supporting Horace Greeley's presidential candidacy. Susan also refuses to support Victoria, causing a rift between Susan and Elizabeth that impacts the NWSA. Ultimately Victoria is nominated for president by the Equal Rights Party with Frederick Douglass chosen as the vice presidential nominee. Although Susan and Elizabeth eventually repair their relationship, Susan's resentment of Victoria remains.

With the YMCA's support for his work, Anthony Comstock is able to be more aggressive in his quest to rid the world of vice and corruption as he defines it. Victoria, Tennie, Freydeh, and Madame Restell are all objects of his fury and determination. It is difficult to feel sympathy for him due to his rabid quest to eliminate everything he considers immoral and his willingness to destroy other people's lives and livelihoods. But Piercy has taken great pains to show us where he came from and how he developed his world view: the "strict hellfire and brimstone sermons" from his childhood (38), the death of his mother when he was young, a father "who never hesitated to take a strap or a stick" to one of his children (130)—all had an impact on him. Piercy also noted her difficulty in writing this character ("I had to struggle to get inside him") and her continued anger at his actions: "You can understand and not forgive" (Lyons 341).

Belfer calls Piercy's delineation of Anthony a "psychologically astute portrait." He is deeply devoted to his wife, primarily because she is as meek and unassuming as he finds appropriate in a woman and because "twice a month she endured the marital embrace without complaint" (205). Anthony is crushed after the unexplainable death of their first baby, and he is troubled by Maggie's apparent inability to successfully bear other children. One day when Anthony is hunting a "purveyor of obscene rubber articles" (307), he encounters a woman about to abandon her dead sister's baby at a church, as she is unable to care for it. He brings the child home for he and Maggie to raise as their own daughter. The doctor tells them that Adele is "slow," but they think she is perfect: "She was gentle, obedient, quiet, shy, everything a girl should be" (338). Anthony drives himself unmercifully, feeling that his job is "fighting evildoers, protecting innocent children and young people from the filth of the streets and the temptations that could corrode that innocence quickly enough "(210). He seems to believe that he can single-handedly save the world from these horrors.

Anthony is successful in getting federal obscenity laws passed—colloquially known as the Comstock Laws—and he is empowered as "an agent of the federal government with broad new powers" and appointed the "secretary of the Society for the Suppression of Vice" (335), which gives him the power to enforce the obscenity laws across the country. He uses stories in an issue of *Woodhull & Claflin's Weekly* as an excuse to arrest Victoria and Tennie, charging them with using the mail to send obscene materials; Victoria is in jail on election day. They are eventually released on bail, but Anthony continues to harass Victoria, dragging her into court several times. However, the scandalous story of Lib Tilton's affair with Henry Ward Beecher has come to public awareness. When Victoria is asked by a reporter if she has "letters written by Henry Ward Beecher that bore upon the case," she says (untruthfully) that she does (325), feeling that this might serve a protective function. Beecher seems to have more influence over the courts than Anthony Comstock, and eventually all the charges against her are dropped.

Victoria has been the support for her entire family and has to find a way to "make money, clear their debts, enable them to live decently again" (327). Accompanied by Tennie, her children, and her mother, she successfully takes to the lecture circuit, first with a speech about healthy sexuality and then with a speech about the Beecher-Tilton case. As the country was growing more conservative, "she began lecturing on her interpretation of the Bible" (359). She begins divorce proceedings against James since she "no longer felt at one with him" and he is doing nothing to support their family or her (359). When Cornelius Vanderbilt dies, his son and heir, William, sends Victoria, Tennie, and the rest of the family to England so they cannot be subpoenaed while other family members contest the will. This opportunity for a fresh start leads Victoria to declare to Tennie that "we're going to be respectable this time" (365). In her effort to return to respectability, Victoria disavows "some of her earlier radical causes such as free love" (380). Although Susan's continued animosity means Victoria is "denied entrance to the women's movement in England," she reaffirms her commitment to women's rights (380).

Anthony also targets Freydeh, and one day when she is selling condoms to a retail outlet, he arrests her "for selling obscene materials" (318). Since she cannot afford both bail and an attorney, Freydeh is in jail for months. Sammy; Sara; and her daughter, Debra, keep the condom business going as best they can in Freydeh's absence, but they have lost customers because "they had been making only the simple cheaper condoms" (351).

Sammy and Freydeh have narrowed down Shaineh's possible location to a "house of assignation" (354). They finally find her, only to watch her die in a physical struggle with Alfred Kumble, the man who "bought and paid for" her (357). After their long search, this sudden tragic outcome hits Freydeh hard. She is able to locate Shaineh's daughter, Reba, and brings her home to join the family she has built, a blend of family by blood and family by choice. Somewhat surprisingly, Asher attacks and lames Kumble in his attempt to "wash away the shame on the family" (390) and to reclaim their honor. It is shame that only Asher feels and, for him, it is aggravated by Reba's presence. He can only see her as the daughter of a prostitute, a characterization Freydeh rejects. Far from agreeing with Asher's description of Reba as "a child of shame," Freydeh claims her as "a sweet little girl who's had a hard time of it" (391). When Asher threatens that he "won't live under the same roof with her" (391), Freydeh tells him to find another place, knowing that he cannot and will not. He is reliant on her, and on her profitable business, to house and feed him and his family. Again, she rejects conventional notions of respectability. Freydeh is satisfied when her business regains its success. "She was the one everyone turned to when there was trouble, when something was needed, she was the one" (392). This also seems true of Victoria and Elizabeth, both of whom take pride in being the center of their families.

Anthony continues chasing pornographers across the country but he is troubled because he has not yet been able to hold Madame Restell accountable; the press, too, has noted his seeming proclivity to go after "the small fry" but leave "the powerful alone" (336). After succeeding in passing new statutes "against abortionists" (368), Anthony arrests Restell. Despite her money and connections, she finds it difficult to make bail because of the notoriety that would attend anyone who would agree to secure her bond. Finally, she is released on bail, goes home, and then commits suicide to protect her family (374) from the scandal of a trial. Although her family is distraught, Anthony is self-righteously satisfied that "her death would serve as a bloody reminder" (375) to others. He feels no regret for the impact of his actions on others.

Susan takes over the daily affairs of the National but Elizabeth is called upon to make speeches in any state that seems likely to pass women's suffrage. After years of working to expand the fight for women's equality beyond suffrage, Elizabeth is frustrated at being reduced to discussing "suffrage, suffrage, suffrage, all the livelong day" (340), contrary to her interests in a broader program of progressive reforms. She becomes more attentive to the impact of poverty and issues of prison reform and she, Susan, and Matilda Gage decide to write a history of the women's movement, parsing out the tasks amongst themselves. Elizabeth observes that as they have been deeply enmeshed in this work for decades, "who could write such a thing if not the three of them" (346).

Piercy ends the novel with a series of short chapters in an epilogue. Here the prose gets even more truncated; Belfer described *Sex Wars* as being "subsumed in a rush of fact, in an attachment to chronology rather than reflection and insight." While this is a somewhat harsh assessment, it certainly seems accurate in this last section. But, the epilogue does allow Piercy to provide closure for her characters.

Elizabeth writes *The Women's Bible,* taking on "religion with a frontal assault" (378), as she believes that "revering a bunch of writing from men who had lived two thousand years ago as holy was ludicrous" (397), an action that "shocked half her allies into distancing themselves" (396).[5] Prior to her death, she reflects with some pleasure on the progress of the women's movement. There has been some progress. Due in no small part to her own efforts, "women were at least on the road to owning themselves," but there was still "much work to do to free woman" (398).

In England, Victoria marries and is later widowed. Finally possessing the respectability she has long coveted, she presides over a country estate, feeling that she makes a difference in the lives of the villagers, although Tennie accuses her of acting the "grande dame" (400). She determines that "someday she would sit down and tell the whole truth for herself as well as for the world" (401), since she has always had to edit and stifle the reality of her experiences. Piercy noted the many different versions of Victoria Woodhull's life that are available and acknowledges that "given her penchant for rewriting her own past, many of the stories and facts are in contradiction" (409). Piercy has chosen "those [versions] I thought likeliest" (409) to ground her own interpretation.

Freydeh has successfully invested in real estate, providing comfort and financial stability for her family. She is quite content, feeling that "she had dragged them all into the middle class . . . she was a matriarch, one without a husband but rich in love and connection" (404). She feels no need for a man, saying to her granddaughter, "What man would let me have my way?" (403). Instead, she has survived and "founded a family" (404).

Anthony Comstock identifies a new enemy in Margaret Sanger, a vocal advocate of family planning and birth control, although the tide of society is turning against him and his quest to rid the country of immorality and evil. When she flees the country, he arrests her husband, who is found guilty of distributing obscene materials; he receives a minimal fine and jail time. Anthony dies of pneumonia, still proud of his work and asking: "Who else could boast as good service to morality?" (408). When Margaret Sanger returns to the States, all charges are dropped.

At one point toward the end of the novel, Elizabeth notes that "the years seemed to move faster and faster" (381), an observation true of the escalating pace of much of this novel as well. Yet, the mad rush through major events in the history of the late-nineteenth century provides enough historical detail and accuracy to give adequate context to the plot of the novel. Should it interest readers to learn more, Piercy has included some of the major reference sources in her Acknowledgments.

Sex Wars encourages readers to think about the connections to present time, similarities that inspired Piercy to write the novel in the first place. In what ways do women's bodies and access to reproductive control continue to be constrained and policed? What is the place of religion in the politics and policies of the nation? When will women's talents and capabilities be more important than their appearance? What family configurations are accepted and protected and which are seen as a challenge to what has been made to seem normal and natural? What changes are required for women to reach full equality in the public and private spheres? Readers might have different answers—but the questions themselves continue to be important.

CHAPTER 4

Imagining the Future

Woman on the Edge of Time and *He, She and It*

Piercy has written two utopian/dystopian novels, *Woman on the Edge of Time* (1976) and *He, She and It* (1991). These novels are particularly significant since, as utopian or speculative fiction, they represent a departure from Piercy's realist novels (although her 1970 *Dance the Eagle to Sleep* foreshadows Piercy's move into the utopian genre). *Woman* is probably the most well-known of Piercy's novels; it appears on course syllabi in women's studies and in science-fiction classes, often alongside Margaret Atwood's *The Handmaid's Tale* (1986). It alternates between the contemporary moment of the novel and the utopic/dystopic possible futures that might be produced as a result of decisions made in that moment. The doubling of characters in the "now" of the book and in the future helps readers trace these points of connection. *He, She and It,* winner of the Arthur C. Clarke Award for Best Science Fiction in the United Kingdom, is set in the middle of the 21st century. Although *Vida* and *Woman* both attend to the military/industrial complex and its use of technology, *He, She and It* is Piercy's most concentrated engagement with science and technology yet. This novel's exploration of what it means to be human and what it means to be a machine is particularly evocative—can Yod, the cyborg, feel emotion? Can Shira, fully human, love a machine? What does this mean for the community in which they live and where Yod was built?

Everything Piercy has written has engaged intentionally with feminist thought/praxis, but *Woman* and *He, She and It* perhaps most overtly operationalize the feminist theories being developed at the times of their writing. For *Woman,* this means the inclusion of radical feminist thought, ecocriticism, feminist perspectives on welfare rights, and the ways in which psychiatric and mental health institutions are used to police and control women and poor people. *He, She and It* is attuned to both cyborg feminism and feminist postmodernism.

Piercy has described *Woman* as "dealing both with the Utopian genre, going back to Plato's *Republic,* and the more recent tradition of feminist utopias" ("Telling Stories" 1). It therefore seems important to articulate some of the ways in which utopian literature functions as a genre in order to have a clear understanding of what Piercy accomplishes with these novels. In her discussion of feminist separatist utopias, Dana Shugar described one function of utopian fiction as "the ways it attempts to envision a better world and advocates action toward the achievement of that world" (xii). Utopian societies are created in literature as alternatives. They develop out of an author's own community/present moment. According to Piercy: "Feminist utopias were created out of a hunger for what we didn't have, at a time when change felt not only possible but probable. Utopias came from the desire to imagine a better society when we dared to do so" ("Woman").

The utopia Piercy has created comes out of her own environment and is intended as an alternative to that society's status quo. It is an implicit and explicit critique of what currently is. In part, utopian literature serves to make visible things that are invisible, sheds light on the hidden assumptions a society takes for granted, and points out the consequences of unarticulated but ever-present societal norms. Peter Ruppert has suggested that utopias "engage us in a dialogue between social fact and utopian dream" (5). Utopian literature has a specific intent; it is not just escapist fiction. It should work to give readers insight into their own communities by offering a new lens through which to view current reality, to suggest alternatives, and to assert that different structural arrangements are possible. At its best, utopian fiction jars us into a new way of seeing. Dystopian fiction accomplishes many of these same things, but through the reverse perspective. In discussing these genres, Piercy insisted that "the point of creating futures is to get people to imagine what they want and don't want to happen down the road—and maybe do something about it" ("Woman"). Where utopian fiction holds out hope for a new and better world we could build and inhabit, dystopian fiction serves as a warning of what will happen if we do not attend to the problematic impulses and practices of our present. Piercy notes that perhaps "*He, She and It* is more relevant today because what I describe in it is happening and happening rapidly" ("Living off the Grid" 50).

Woman slips seamlessly between three different genres: utopian fiction, dystopian fiction, and social realism. The novel's protagonist, Connie Ramos, is a poor, overweight, middle-aged Chicana woman living in New York City. These identity characteristics should signal to readers that this story will be different; Connie is not the kind of protagonist we often see in literature. The story opens with her niece Dolly seeking shelter at Connie's apartment after Dolly's pimp Geraldo has beaten her in response to the news that she is pregnant with his child. Soon Geraldo appears with a quack doctor to force Dolly to have an abortion. After smashing a bottle in Geraldo's face in an attempt to protect Dolly, Connie is taken to Bellevue Hospital. Dolly verifies Geraldo's version of what happened and joins him in blaming Connie for instigating the fracas. When Connie later asks why she lied, Dolly responds: "He is my man . . . What can I do?" (24).

During Connie's intake interview at Bellevue, her prior history of hospitalization at Rockover State, a psychiatric institution, is discussed. Connie's lover, Claud, a blind musician and pickpocket, died in jail as a result of a medical experiment which involved his being injected with hepatitis. In her pain and grief, Connie self-medicated with alcohol and drugs, causing her to ignore the needs of her four-year old daughter, Angelina. At one point, frustrated with her inability to adequately provide for Angelina, and "hung over and strung out" (62), Connie hits her, resulting in Angelina's broken wrist. As a result, Connie loses custody of Angelina; her parental rights are terminated and Angelina is quickly adopted away from her. Immersed in self-hatred and contempt, she agrees to be sent to Rockover; "they said I was sick and I agreed" (25).

After the incident with Geraldo, her brother Lewis signs the commitment papers and she is sent again, this time over her objections, from Bellevue back to Rockover State. Connie's experience at Rockover makes clear how deeply dysfunctional the mental health system is. There appears to be little interest in actually treating any mental health conditions at Rockover, and more interest in simply managing and controlling patient behavior or asserting staff power over the patients. M. Keith Booker noted that "*Woman on the Edge of Time* presents Piercy's contemporary America as a society that is already a dystopia for marginal members of society like her protagonist, Connie Ramos" (339). Barely able to survive financially, and ignored by those making decisions about her, Connie seems to have little ability to change the conditions of her life.

Before Dolly arrives at her apartment in distress, Connie has begun seeing a young man in her dreams who tells her his name is Luciente. He soon appears in front of her on a city sidewalk. Connie first believes she might be hallucinating and then becomes fearful that he will attack or rob her. She cannot imagine what else he might want with her. Luciente says that her "mind is unusual" and that she is "a catcher, a receptive" (41). She thinks he must be crazy. But, when Connie takes the subway home, she acknowledges that he is right about the "receptive part. Queasy things happened in her . . . [knowing] things about others she should not know" (43). Lonely that evening, she decides to do what he has asked and see what happens if she does think of him.

When Luciente arrives, Connie wants to know: "How do you get in here?" (52). Luciente tells her something unbelievable: he is from the year 2137, in the future, from a village called Mattapoisett. She is not hallucinating; it is some kind of experimental psychic contact. Of course, Connie finds this ludicrous, but also finds herself distracted by his questions about her time and curious about his explanations of his future. Their conversation is interrupted when Dolly bangs on her door seeking refuge from Geraldo.

At Rockover, heavily medicated and placed in seclusion after attempting to refuse medication, Connie encounters Luciente again. Luciente is taken aback by the conditions of Connie's "loony bin" (65), telling her that, unlike her surroundings, the madhouses in his village are pleasant and are "places where people retreat when they want to go down into themselves" (66). Connie informs him that here, mental hospitals are for people no one wants.

Luciente proposes taking Connie to see his village, warning her that the suggestion is an experiment; he doesn't actually know if it can really be done. But, as they stand near each other, Connie is shocked to discover that Luciente is a woman. She quickly realizes why she misidentified Luciente's gender. Luciente speaks and moves with confidence and authority, she takes up "more space than women ever did," she doesn't worry "about how her body is displayed" (67). One benefit to realizing that Luciente is female is that Connie is not afraid of her anymore. They successfully transition to Luciente's village, Mattapoisett.

Connie is not sure what it will be like, but she certainly expects some kind of sophisticated technology. She is shocked, and somewhat disappointed, to see so much she recognizes: a river, small buildings, bicycles, clothes hanging to dry, gardens, goats, a rooster. It looks to her just like her uncle's home in poverty-stricken, rural Texas. Luciente is upset at Connie's reaction, because "we like it this way!" Luciente soon optimistically decides that Connie will like it better "when you see more" (70). Luciente tries to demonstrate for Connie the difference that exists between involuntary poverty and deprivation and a voluntary and intentional social structure developed in congruence with a community's beliefs, where everyone has what they need. Interestingly, in a 1977 interview, Piercy suggested that Mattapoisett is not, in fact, a utopia, because everything in is available now: "There's almost nothing there except the brooder not accessible now. So it's hardly a utopia; it is very intentionally not a utopia because it is not strikingly new. The ideas are the ideas basically of the women's movement" ("An Interview with *Sandscript*" 100). Even though Mattapoisett's societal structures and ideals are rooted in feminist thought, embedding them in a novel designed for a broader public means that, for many readers, these ideas *will* be new.

The narrative strategy of having Connie visit Mattapoissett provides a mechanism for Luciente to explain their way of life and how their social and political systems operate. The dualisms and binary thinking that structure contemporary Connie's present have been imploded. Descriptive categories exist—male/female, adult/children, black/white—but they do not carry the same meaning or limitations that Connie experiences. They do not create or reinforce power differentials. With this, *Woman* anticipates Audre Lorde's later analysis of difference, demonstrating that difference itself is not the problem. The problem is "the distortions which have resulted from the ignoring and misnaming of those differences" (Lorde 122).

In Mattapoisett, there are no gendered pronouns in use—rather than he or she, everyone is "per" (63). Individuals are not privileged because one is a man or disempowered because one is a woman; everyone is valued as a human, a person; correspondingly, there is no need to deny or suppress individuality.

People choose their own family groups; the nuclear family is no longer a unit of procreation. Connie finds herself shocked and almost repulsed when she sees the means of reproduction and learns how children are parented. Luciente takes her to meet Bee, one of Luciente's "sweet friends" (65), who works in the "brooder" where embryos are grown (101). As one example of Piercy's choice to provide doubled characters, Bee reminds Connie of her former lover, Claud. Bee tells Connie that although they have chosen to maintain separate "cultural identities" for a rich diversity, genes are mixed and distributed "through the population" (104). He emphasizes that they "broke the bond between genes and culture, broke it forever. We want there to be no chance of racism again" (104).

In Mattapoisett, there is a firm and intentional rejection of biological essentialism. Sexuality is not tied to reproduction and there is no identifiable genetic link between parents and their children. There is also a distinction between childbirth and childrearing; in Mattapoisett they are not connected and therefore do not serve the same social function. Children are "born" from the brooder. The three comothers or coms who raise a child can be men or women. Usually, though, coms are not also "sweet friends" in order to protect the child from getting 'caught in love misunderstandings" (74). Hormones are used so the men can breastfeed too. Gender is not relevant to the identity of mother. Connie is frustrated, exclaiming "How can men be mothers? How can some kid who isn't related to you be your child?" Luciente explains: "It was part of women's long revolution. When we were breaking all the old hierarchies. Finally there was that one thing we had to give up too, the only power we ever had, in return for no more power for anyone. The original production: the power to give birth. Cause as long as we were biologically enchained, we'd never be equal. And males never would be humanized to be loving and tender. So we all became mothers. Every child has three. To break the nuclear bonding" (105).

Piercy has pushed readers to ask: What does it mean to be a woman and how does childbearing relate to that meaning? What is the social value of gendered motherhood and live birth? Do we have to be mothers to be real women? Do we have to be women to be real mothers? What would the relationship between men and women need to be for reproductive technology, and access to that technology, to be not an object of struggle controlled by a capitalist patriarchal medical system, but instead a social practice grounded in equality?

In her imagined system of reproduction, Piercy evokes the ground-breaking work of Shulamith Firestone, whose book, *The Dialectic of Sex: The Case for Feminist Revolution,* argued for the need to end the "sex class" system (11). For Firestone, one of the key components to ending the sex class system which perpetuates gender inequality is: "the development of a technology capable of freeing women from the tyranny of their sexual-reproductive roles—both the fundamental biological condition itself, and the sexual class system built upon, and reinforcing, this biological condition" (37). Firestone specifies that she means both "artificial reproduction" and "cybernetics" (190). Although Connie's first glance at Mattapoisett leads her to believe it is not an advanced society, there is in fact a very sophisticated apparatus that maintains the community, even at the level of reproduction, a process which seems natural and instinctive.

Connie is initially furious at this practice, feeling that she "hated them, the bland bottleborn monsters of the future, born without pain, multi-colored like a litter of puppies without the stigmata of race and sex" (106). But she comes to see how children are valued and integrated throughout the community. There are no artificial "toys for teaching sex roles to children" (138); children learn by doing. One of the things they learn is that gender and sex roles do not determine actions and responsibilities. Although each child has comothers, everyone helps teach and raise the children; everyone helps them grow and develop. Luciente's daughter, Dawn, evokes Connie's own daughter, Angelina, another doubling of characters. Connie comes to realize how different life would have been if Angelina could have been raised in such a loving community where everyone has enough nurturing, affection, food, education, and support (141), where Angelina was not totally dependent on the limited resources Connie could provide. Connie sees how different it would be for herself as well: "In Mattapoisett she too would have respect. And learning." (215). The possibilities of who and what she could be would not be restricted by individual economic capacity.

In the future, people's names have no gender connotations and no connection to patriarchal lineage (77). Although children are given a name at birth, they later choose their own names as part of a ritual to mark adulthood, sometimes cycling through several names before they decide on one. This practice is not unfamiliar to Connie as she thinks of her own different names: "I've always had three names inside me." She was named Consuelo, then used Connie when she "managed to get two years of college," and she was Conchita during her most self-destructive period (122). In this way, Connie, too, has chosen names, or different versions of her name, to indicate who she has been at any given point in her life.

Part of the Mattapoisset ritual enabling the transition into adulthood involves each child living alone in the wilderness as a way to break "dependencies" on others and achieve full membership into society (116). Bee's daughter Innocente is undertaking this journey. When she learns of it, Connie is shocked at the custom, seeing it as abandoning a child to danger. Innocente, however, is outraged at the implication that she cannot take care of herself adequately: "I know what to eat in the woods! I'm twelve and a half, not four" (116). When Innocente returns from her time in the woods, her former comothers are not allowed to speak to her for three months. This helps to interrupt any remaining patterns of dependency or control and is an intentional effort to provide space for Innocente, who returns as Hawk, to strengthen her new status as an adult and become a full and equal member of the community.

Mattapoisset is just one of the many communities that exist in the future. In some ways, these communities function like states or countries, but without overarching nation-state bureaucracy, territoriality, or defense mechanisms against each other. Each community works to be self-sufficient. Luciente says that "every region tries to be ownfed" (70), but each also exports the surplus items they produce (128). Luciente shares the list of Mattapoisset's exports with Connie, which include: food; plants and seeds; diving equipment; cultural products; and more (128). Representatives of each community move from place to place to share information. Each person and every community has their own space, but property is held in common. There is a planning council for each region, and a central decision-making body—grandcil—at which each unit has representation and equal voice.

Everything at Mattapoisset has been carefully planned with robust community participation and deliberation. The community thinks deeply about quality of life issues and is also committed to living lightly on the earth. Jackrabbit tells Connie, "we care a lot how things are done" (130). Conservation and sustainability are important factors in any decisions that are made. Technology is used to benefit people, not for profit, the accumulation of wealth, or the manufacture of expensive objects. Society has been structured by reflecting on deep, philosophical questions that impact daily life, such as what does it mean to work? What does work do for a person and a community? What is surplus value, what do you do with it and who gets to decide? What is the value of time? How are objects produced and distributed? The decisions that are made are not static and are frequently deliberated and discussed. Nothing is fixed, or unable to be questioned or changed. As Luciente says, "we'd change it if we didn't like it, how not? We're always changing things around" (70).

It is not only how society, government, or work are organized that receive attention; maintaining healthy interpersonal relationships is also of concern to everyone. When Luciente and Bolivar "are picky toward each other's ways" (207) as a result of both of them loving Jackrabbit, resulting in a seemingly rare expression of jealousy and competition, there is a "worming" where several community members meet with the three of them to "try to comprend that hostility and see if we can defuse it" (207). This is a productive, community-based strategy for dealing with interpersonal conflict. Connie cannot quite understand this practice—she asks, "don't you people have nothing to worry about besides personal stuff?" (207)—but there is widespread agreement that attending to signs of conflict in interpersonal relationships early on is an important investment of time, and key to the smooth running of the community. Parra, the referee, notes that "they need not like each other to behave civilly" (207). Luciente and Bolivar are willing to participate in the worming because they are committed both to Jackrabbit and to the success of their community.

As Connie spends more and more time at Mattapoisett, Luciente tells her that they "are only one possible future" (177) and much of the ability for their future to manifest depends on what happens in Connie's time. Connie encounters one of the other possible futures when she tries to access Luciente and Mattapoisett on her own initiative and instead ends up in Gildina's world. Gildina lives in a climate-controlled tower and is contracted to a security guard, Cash, who is owned by a "multi" (299), a corporate structure seen again in *He, She and It*. He provides room, board, and other support and she provides him with sex. She seems to Connie like a "cartoon of femininity" (288) as her body has been "cosmetically fixed for sex use" (299), altered by cosmetic surgery, genetic manipulation and recurring "beauty-ops" (288). Cash has "sharpened control" (297) and has been altered to be a "fighting machine" (299), almost a cyborg. Gildina's world is clearly intended to be a cautionary tale about a future where the environment has been destroyed, corporations and "richies" (298) control everything and everyone. It is the opposite of Mattapoisett, but a dystopia all too imaginable from Connie's time.

The other possible future Connie encounters finds her with Luciente, Bee, Otter, and Hawk at the front on defense, first on the ground fighting the enemy, "tall figures entirely encased in seamless metallic uniforms" (220)—and then in a floater shooting at their opponent's "khaki floaters" (336), one of which seems to be populated by the doctors who are experimenting on Connie in her own time. While they are waiting for the ground troops to approach, Otter recites a poem she has just written, inspired by a beautiful maple leaf. Connie finds this odd, asking "how can you write poems about leaves now," but Otter finds it "natural" at a moment when they might be "close to death" (330). Hawk is singing as she pilots the floater. The lyrics are hopeful: "an army of lovers cannot lose" (333). The scene is another example of how integrated life is in the Mattapoisett future; the arts do not exist separate from the rest of the world and anyone can make art when and as they wish.

Connie learns about positive and enriching uses of technology at Mattapoisett, as well as the misuse of technology in the frightening possible future that Gildina foreshadows. In Connie's world, science and technology are about power and control. In her own present, Connie is struggling to protect herself against a team of doctors who are engaged in medical experiments. They are surgically implanting electrodes to stimulate portions of the brain, purportedly to cure the "poor impulse control" (199) that landed patients at Rockford in the first place. In fact, "deep brain stimulation" through "neural implants" became popular in the 1960s and 1970s and, for some time, was seen by law enforcement as a potential mechanism to control the "violent tendencies" that they believed caused crime and social unrest (Slater 65), so Piercy was drawing on recent history for these plot developments. It's clear to Connie that she and the other patients are all just guinea pigs in service to the career aspirations of the doctors involved. She is terrified at the thought that they are going to put something in her brain that she cannot control and that will change who she is. She tries to escape to avoid the surgery, but is unsuccessful and subsequently returned to Rockford. After the patients involved in the experiment are moved to a new psychiatric facility, a dialytrode and drugs are implanted in Connie's brain. She is constantly trying to figure out how she can resist what is being done to her. Luciente and Bee encourage her to consider herself "a prisoner of war" and to continue to fight, Bee advising that "there's always a thing you can deny an oppressor" (328). This is a lesson in the struggle for social justice. There is always an intervention, however small, that one can make.

Connie's visits to the future manifest to the doctors and nurses on the ward as her becoming unconscious, for hours at a time. As a patient in an experiment, this causes great concern. When the doctors alter her medication, they postpone the other surgeries, which Connie considers her "first victory" (325). The second time her lengthy unconsciousness worries them, the dialytrode is temporarily removed. Connie then begins to behave in ways the medical team finds acceptable in order to make them believe the brain surgery and the technology they installed was the problem. She performs compliance, she helps other patients, she initiates conversation, and she expresses interest in her appearance. This is all part of her tactical strategy; Connie acknowledges she is "at war" (338). Rather than feeling helpless and unable to do anything to impact her situation, she is intentional and strategic.

Connie tries to get out of the hospital, hoping to find a way to escape and disappear before the doctors can operate on her again. She is persistent in her attempts to convince her brother Luis, Dolly's father, to let her come and visit on Thanksgiving by offering to help his third wife, Adele, with all the chores preparing for and cleaning up from the holiday. Although Luis eventually agrees, she is carefully supervised during her visit and locked in her bedroom at night. The day after Thanksgiving, Luis takes her to his business—a plant nursery with greenhouses—to help. In a rare moment when she is left alone, she steals one of the pesticides—the deadly parathion. After Luis returns her to the hospital, Connie makes one last visit to Mattapoisett where Luciente notes the "hardness" in her mind. Connie must close herself off from their connection, from friendship and community, "to kill someone with power over me" (370). After an unsuccessful conversation with the doctors trying to convince them not to operate on her again, Connie intentionally poisons their coffee. Four of the medical team die as a result of Connie's actions.

What is the purpose of Connie's deadly action? Why does she kill? Booker noted that "there is certainly some question as to the political effectiveness of this multiple murder" and suggested that it might signal "an indictment of a system that insists so blindly on defining Ramos as violent and dangerous that it eventually makes her that way" (341). However, although it's an act that seems contrary to Connie's ethos, in some ways it might be a rational choice. In her experience, when there is evidence that the medical experiments are producing unwelcome results, they are at least halted. Perhaps she chooses murder in an effort to delay them. Perhaps she is following Bee's advice and intervening in an oppressive and terrifying situation in the only way she can find. In "Splittings," Adrienne Rich writes of "choosing something new / not to suffer uselessly" (23–24). Perhaps this is the choice Connie makes as well. Perhaps she is done with being a pawn in a system she cannot impact and decides to exhibit her agency by acting, even as she faces certain punishment as a result of those actions. Perhaps Connie consciously decides to commit violence and face the consequences of continued confinement in the hope that her actions will save others.

The novel ends with notes from her medical file that make clear how the mental health system has pathologized Connie's daily life. Through these notes we can see "the official ideology of the medical establishment and of the social values it represents" (Booker 340). The critique of the mental health system in Piercy's novel is similar to the conclusions in Phyllis Chesler's *Women and Madness.* In part, Chesler explored the ways in which women's actions are policed and interpreted as deviant if they fall outside of a very narrow window of what is seen as appropriate feminine behavior. Once labeled mentally ill, they are warehoused into institutions where their behavior can be monitored, punished and/or controlled. Lisa Maria Hogeland has noted that "attacks on conventional, patriarchal psychiatry and psychology abound in the feminist theory of the early 1970s" (27).

In *Woman on the Edge of Time,* Piercy showed Connie's transformation as she moved from the individual frustration, anger, and resignation she feels as a result of the injustices she experiences to a deep understanding of the systemic bases of her oppression. This shift in perspective leads to her feeling empowered to take action on behalf of herself and others. Hogeland describes this recognition as "Connie's process of consciousness raising" (116). Bee told Connie earlier that "often even with vastly unequal power, you can find or force an opening to fight back" (328). Washing her hands after poisoning the coffee, Connie says to herself "I'm a dead woman now too. I know it. But I did fight them. I'm not ashamed. I tried" (375). She doesn't know what the ultimate results or consequences of her action will be, beyond the deaths, but she has resisted in the only way she could "because it is war" (375). Sadly, the only avenue Connie can find to assert some control over her life is one that will result in continued confinement and surveillance.

In *He, She and It,* a war of resistance is also being fought. In this novel, Piercy revisited and expanded issues that were central to *Woman on the Edge of Time.* She reworked many of the same binary oppositions she unpacked in *Woman*—man/woman, youth/age, science-technology/nature, childbearing/childrearing—bringing in cyborgs and Jewish mysticism to enhance her discussion. This novel foregrounds sexuality and gender politics, the role of mothering, separatist societies, questions of literacy—including orality and computer literacy, ecofeminism, and ageism, as well as a reworking of the creation debate reminiscent of Mary Shelley's *Frankenstein,* a text referenced in *He, She and It.* Piercy's story serves as a compelling warning about what can or will happen—what is happening—in the contemporary race for technological superiority with an increasingly stratified social and economic structure; and with seemingly immutable power hierarchies—at the expense of human connection.

In the acknowledgments to *He, She and It,* Piercy noted the impact of Donna Haraway's important essay, "A Manifesto for Cyborgs," on her novel. Haraway invoked the image of the cyborg—a blend of human and machine—in connection with her examination of the increased power of science and technology; she imagined the cyborg as a site of possibility in transgressing boundaries and moving away from identity politics and towards a politics of affinity. She wrote: "a cyborg world might be about lived social and bodily realities in which people are not afraid of their joint kinship with animals and machines, not afraid of permanently partial identities and contradictory standpoints" (154). For Haraway, "there are also great riches for feminists in explicitly embracing the possibilities inherent in the breakdown of clean distinctions between organism and machine and similar distinctions structuring the Western self" (174). Haraway—and Piercy—is disrupting the imposed difference between human and machine. Haraway credits many authors of science fiction for "exploring what it means to be embodied in high-tech worlds" (173), as Piercy has done here.

Although a critical apparatus has slowly developed around *He, She and It,* for many years it was relatively unnoticed by the literary establishment. Peter Fitting remarks that "the novel has received little or no attention within the North American science fiction community, even after it won the Arthur C. Clarke award as the best science fiction novel of 1992 in Great Britain" (4). Piercy commented on this oversight, noting of *He, She and It* that, "of all my novels, this one—one of the most ambitious and complex—received the fewest reviews in the feminist press, because of its genre" ("Foreword" x), not to mention its lack of attention in mainstream press. Piercy observed that when *He, She and It* won the Clarke award, "my American publisher would not sticker the books [denoting its award-winning status] for fear winning this prize would actually hurt sales" (x).

The novel begins in the twenty-first century in the middle of a child custody battle. Shira Shipman loses custody of her young son Ari to her ex-husband Josh Rogovin. Josh and Shira both work for Y-S, one of the "twenty-three great multis" (3), corporate amalgamations that rule the world. After winning custody, Josh attempts to completely sever the relationship between Ari and Shira by taking Ari to Pacifica, a space platform. Since Shira has no access to her child and no avenue of appeal, she decides to accept a job in her hometown of Tikva and retreats there to consider her options. Tikva is a "free town" (3) which exists independently of any corporate control, although it is under constant threat of attack and takeover. One of the ways it preserves its independence is by contracting to many different multis for highly technical and specialized computer programs, invoking the capitalist protection of meeting insatiable demand with unique products others cannot supply.

Shira is hired by Avram, an old family friend and the father of her first lover, Gadi, to help him with his latest experiment. Avram is building intelligent robots which resemble humans, in contravention of the "corporate covenants" forbidding this activity (49). Robots are supposed to be clearly identifiable as non-human and programmed for limited functioning only. Instead, Avram secretly creates cyborgs. Avram built Yod, his latest cyborg, in part to protect Tikva from both physical intruders and information pirates. Yod is an anatomically male "fusion of machine and lab-created biological components" who looks human (70). His capabilities are impressive: "Yod has extensive cybernetic, mathematical and systems analysis programming, probability theory, up-to-date scientific knowledge of an encyclopedic width. He is also programmed with general history, forty languages, Torah, Talmud, halakic law" (70). Shira is needed to acculturate Yod, to educate him "in how to speak to humans, how to behave socially, how to handle his functions" (71). Avram is convinced that Yod must pass as human in order to perform his duties. Avram has "programmed him to protect us—our town, its inhabitants, our Base" (70). Yod's convincing performance as human also protects Avram from repercussions for building him illegally in the first place.

Avram's experiments with cyborgs had started years ago. When Shira and Gadi were teenagers, they discovered that Avram was creating an unusual kind of robot. Shira was surprised when she saw it: "She had never seen a robot shaped like a person. It was illegal to make one that way, just as it was illegal to create robots with human-level intelligence" (46). Her own house computer later explains to her the history of the prohibition on building intelligent, human-looking robots, which exists because "people sometimes fear intelligent machines" (48). After Shira and Gadi discover Avram's secret, he calls on them at times when he needs help with his experiments. He names each version after the letters in the Hebrew alphabet. Yod is the culmination of the project—Avram calls him "*The* cyborg" (69).

Avram created Yod in human form, noting that "I frequently had to sacrifice efficiency to a convincing façade and behavior" (71). However, it is Shira's grandmother, Malkah, who has given him much of the programming that allows him to successfully pass as human, including the capacity for sexual desire. She programmed in "the equivalent of an emotional side . . . a need for bonding . . . a positive reaction to novelty . . . curiosity was a given for him" (351). Malkah explains Yod's programming to Shira: "Avam made him male—entirely so. Avram thought that was the ideal: pure reason, pure logic, pure violence. The world has barely survived the males we have running around. I gave him a gentler side, starting with emphasizing his love for knowledge and extending it to emotional and personal knowledge, a need for connection" (142). Yod is also programmed "to be self-correcting . . . given the ability to reprogram himself" (351).

As Shira works to socialize Yod, she begins to relate to him as if he is a person. Still, she is shocked when Yod reveals that he desires her sexually. The revelation occurs when Gadi, now a famous designer of the immersive virtual reality experiences called stimmies, returns to Tikva in disgrace after being flogged for having sex with a fifteen-year-old girl. Shira has not seen much of Gadi since they were adolescents; she left for college after their very painful breakup, a breakup instigated by Gadi who orchestrated a situation where Shira would discover him having sex with one of their classmates. At that point in their lives, he wanted to build some distance between them, "to know other people, to find out who I am and who they are" (56). After they visit Gadi in the hospital, Yod tells Shira that Gadi "wants you" (130). He equates his desire for Shira with Gadi's noting that "the wanting is the same" (130). Shira is first in disbelief, thinking "I am not hearing what I think I am hearing" (130). How can a machine feel sexual desire? But, she is also curious.

In the discussion that follows Yod's confession, Yod exhibits what Shira calls "a magnificent adolescent funk" (151) as he compares himself to the monster built by Dr. Frankenstein, a connection he makes after Gadi refers to him as "the Son of Frankenstein" (148). Seeking to comfort him, Shira notes the blurriness of boundaries between human and machine, pointing out how little difference exists between her and Yod. People have retinal implants, artificial organs, computer interfaces. Shira says, "we're all unnatural now. . . .we're all cyborgs" (150). He is a machine with human traits; she is a human with technological enhancements. From her perspective at the moment, there is not a significant distinction.

The now of *He, She and It* is interspersed with a story Malkah tells Yod in episodes "through the Base" (18). The Base is both a way of virtually connecting in real time and a mechanism for leaving information for another to retrieve at their convenience. In Malkah's tale, Piercy invoked what Alden Oreck identified as the "most well-known story of the golem." Although Adam is briefly referred to as a golem briefly in the Talmud, Piercy instead reclaimed the story of Rabbi Judah Loew, a historical figure also known as the Maharal of Prague, who uses his "skill and knowledge of the Kabbalah" (Michaelson) to create a golem. The golem, Benjamin Kerstein claimed, is "the most famous and enduring of all Jewish legends." Regarding its continuing popularity, Piercy shared: the "story of the golem that I used in *He, She and It,* I first heard from my grandmother" (*Sleeping* 34). She has reenvisioned the story of Rabbi Loew, noting that in many versions of the legend he "was generally rendered into a figure of a wonder-working Hasidic rabbi. But that wasn't who Judah Loew was" ("Telling Stories" 2). Piercy explained that she "did a great deal of research on Rabbi Loew and his circle and the Prague of his time" (Weinbaum 101). She "thought his historical presence as an intellectual of the Renaissance . . . was fascinating. I did not wish to simplify him" (2). For Piercy, retelling the story of this golem was as much about its creator as about the golem itself.

Piercy created a parallel between the creation story of Joseph and that of Yod, reminiscent of her doubling of characters in *Woman*. Joseph was created by the Maharal in the 1600s to protect the Jews of Prague from Christian prejudice and violence; Yod was created by Avram in the middle of the 21st century to protect Tikva against the multis. Haraway noted the importance of creation narratives, arguing that feminist politics need to attend to "the systems of myth and meanings structuring our imaginations" (163). She suggested that "in retelling origin stories, cyborg authors subvert the central myths of origin of Western culture" (175). This is not the Biblical story of Adam and Eve, the pursuit of knowledge and the subsequent loss of innocence. Piercy's creation stories have problematized an origin myth based on the reliance of some notion of organic wholeness; both Yod and Joseph are hybrid beings.

There are similarities in the ways the Maharal and Avram interact with their creations. The Maharal "speaks more coldly to Joseph" than to others (82), marking him as different from humans. Joseph notices this, stating: "you talk to me differently than you talk to anyone else" (260). Although in Joseph's mind, the Maharal created him, the Maharal is angered when Joseph calls him "Father," saying curtly "you should not call me Father . . . You should call me Rabbi" (81). Joseph is the answer to the question which is ever on the Maharal's mind: "How can he save the Jews of Prague" (25). The Maharal is told in a vision to make the golem, who "is to become a one-man army" (27–28), to protect them. There is no question in the Maharal's mind about Joseph's status. He is a tool; nothing more.

Initially Yod too refers to Avram as "my father" (73). After he begins to learn more about humans and how they behave, Yod no longer sees Avram as his father. Rather he sees their relationship as "one of unequal power . . . He's more my judge than my father" (120). Shira notices that Yod speaks "more precisely, more coldly" to Avram than to others (126), perhaps in an effort to create a barrier between them where Yod can maintain some semblance of privacy and agency. Avram also sees Yod as a tool to protect Tikva, but he has designed him to have human qualities.

The person who spends time with and humanizes Joseph is Chava, the Maharal's granddaughter. She answers his questions about people, helping him learn how to act and interact with others, as Shira is doing with Yod. At Joseph's request, she begins to teach him to read. Being conversant with the kabbalah and other ancient texts, Chava suspects what he is but finds his status irrelevant, saying to Joseph, "whatever you are, you are not less than a man" (113). Joseph recognizes that he loves Chava. When he shares this with Chava, she gently responds that she is not interested in an intimate relationship with anyone, but asks for his friendship, promising in return that she "will be a true friend" (293).

The Maharal is not angry when he learns that Joseph is learning to read as he believes that "even the poorest child should learn to read and write, should learn Hebrew" (203). He also recognizes the benefit of Joseph's literacy: "you are more useful when you can read signs" (204). In this, we see a similarity to one of the most important guiding philosophies of Tikva: "everyone in Tikva was equipped with interface . . . equipped to access the Net directly, heir to all the knowledge of the ages" (55). As Shira's mother Riva says later in the novel, "information shouldn't be a commodity. That's obscene" (194). Everyone should have access to knowledge and information.

A different origin myth attaches to Shira. Shira has virtually no relationship with her mother Riva. Riva doesn't live in Tikva and Shira has rarely seen her; Malkah has raised Shira since she was small. This practice, Shira has been told, is a long-standing family tradition; when a woman has a child, she gives the child to her mother (the child's grandmother) to raise and care for (11, 14). Shira's recollection of Riva is as a "dowdy prematurely middle-aged woman"; Shira "never quite grasped what her mother did, but obviously nothing important" (14). We learn early on that this assessment is inaccurate. In telling Yod the golem story, Malkah likens herself to the Maharal as each has been "a poor parent and a fine grandparent" (22). Malkah then says of her daughter: "I have raised an outlaw who operates far from me with a price on her head" (22). Readers learn later what she means by that.

When Malkah learns that Riva is coming to Tikva incognito, she is compelled to tell Shira the truth about Riva's work: "Riva is an information pirate, Shira. She finds hidden knowledge and liberates it. . . . Your mother is a political fugitive" (78–79). Shira is in disbelief and then immediately worries that Riva might be coming to take Ari, being unaware that Ari is not with Shira; Shira then learns that Malkah fabricated "that little myth about our family to explain to you why you were being raised by me instead of your mother" (79). This information calls into question for Shira everything she has believed about her life; however, it also helps her understand why "Y-S devalued me" (79). They knew, even if Shira did not, that her mother was "a dangerous criminal" (79) and probably limited her career advancement as a result. In this same conversation, Shira learns more about her grandmother as a person. Unlike storybook grandmothers; "her grandmother danced like a prima ballerina through the webs of artificial intelligence and counted herself to sleep with worry beads of old lovers" (79). Shira finds this slightly disconcerting. But, all the Shipman women are unusual in different ways.

Prior to Riva's visit to Tikva, Malkah is attacked in Base and is saved by Yod from death or from having her "brain rendered passive as a sponge" (144). This attack means that "the Base was no longer secure" (156), something almost unfathomable. Although she recovers physically, Malkah remains afraid to re-enter the Base and thus feels useless and no longer herself. The chapter "Malkah's Bed Song" (158) is a reflection on that fear and on the course of her life, which she has lived fully and on her own terms. She reflects on her reasons for seducing Yod, which was "a lovely way to end my sex life" (162), and on the impact of the attack on her capabilities.

In the Base or the Net, Malkah is ageless: "What is physical aging to a base-spinner?" (161); there, she can be anyone: any age, any gender, any persona she wishes. In contrast, after the attack, "I am reduced to my aging body in my room" (161). Yod finds and kills Malkah's attackers in the Net, rendering it safe for her to enter again. The news that she can access the Base and the Net again is rejuvenating for Malkah. She recognizes how important her work is to her: "I like a good hard job that matters" (174)—she likes to be useful.

The discovery that the raiders were sent by Y-S, Shira's former employer, is very troubling. In addition, one of them was Zee, a former student of Malkah's, something that leaves her feeling both sad and betrayed. This news means that "everything will have to be restructured" (166)—their physical security; cybersecurity; and their safety and defense practices and protocols must all be re-engineered. Since Zee had lived in Tikva, everything has likely been compromised.

Shira welcomes physical intimacy with Yod immediately after this. He is hesitant at first, wondering if she is only willing "because I cleared the Base of danger," but Shira reassures him that reward is not her motivation: "I'm doing it because I want to" (168). Shira is surprised at the depth of her sexual response to Yod, but also very pleased and satisfied. Malkah warns Yod not to let Shira know that they too had been lovers. Again, Yod wonders about motivation: "Are you ashamed?" Malkah quickly denies this but notes that "Shira would be shocked. . . . She's more conventional than I am" (172). Certainly Shira has not yet been as sexually curious or adventurous as Malkah, although her choice to take a cyborg as lover does indicate a level of daring.

As Shira and Yod continue their relationship, Shira realizes that in some ways he is very different from a fully human man. Although certainly he sees gender, it doesn't signify in the same way to him as to others. It doesn't require a particular set of responses or actions. Shira finds that when she "moved into her usual behavior with men," Yod does not react as she has grown to expect. In fact, "whole sets of male-female behavior simply did not apply" (245). For example, when Shira dresses up for a party, he cannot understand that her fancy dress marks a special occasion. She asks what he thinks of it, wondering if he finds that "this dress is attractive" and "a little sexy" (244), clearly angling for a compliment. Yod is unable to oblige, acknowledging that "one set of clothing is like another to me. That doesn't appear as comfortable" (243). Although at first slightly hurt by this lack of response, Shira recognizes the benefits of having a partner who has not been socialized to react in patriarchal ways. Not having to perform conventional femininity, not having to be concerned with externally-imposed standards of beauty and behavior, becomes freeing for Shira.

It does not take Y-S long to respond to the death of their raiders. Shira is soon contacted with a request to meet because her "appeal on the custody of Ari had been reconsidered" (176). Malkah immediately recognizes this as a pretext, but Y-S knows Shira's vulnerability; Ari is her weak spot. Shira is unwilling to acknowledge a connection between the attack and this offer: "I have to go. . . . Maybe the attack on the Base comes from an entirely different arm of Y-S" (176). But whether to attend the meeting is not a decision only for Shira. Since Tikva has been attacked, the Base Overseers and the Town Council must be consulted. It is determined that Shira will go and that she "should use the negotiations" to try to figure out "what Y-S wants" (177), although everyone suspects a trap. Yod, of course, will accompany her for protection and safety.

While the arrangements for the Y-S meeting are being made, Riva arrives in disguise as a complaining, dissatisfied old woman accompanied by her nurse. Riva is pretending to be Malkah's sister, Shira's great-aunt Dalia. As soon as they enter the house, it is clear how deep their disguise is. The house notes that "the two persons who have just entered are extremely augmented. Both have considerable internal circuitry for combat and communication" (187). The meeting between Shira and Riva is stilted and uncomfortable. Riva acknowledges that she has "been as rotten a daughter as I am a mother" but hopes that "you and I can manage to make friends with each other before I have to leave" (189). Riva's companion is revealed as Nili who identifies herself as "an assassin" (189), an identity that seems very likely given her skills and abilities. Her physical capacities are so impressive that Shira is compelled to ask "Is she human?" (190). When Nili describes Yod as "a machine" (195), Yod retorts that Nili is "part machine and part human yourself" (195), a conversation which reinforces Shira's earlier argument that they are all cyborgs. Nili comes from an interdicted land in the former Middle East which everyone believes uninhabitable because of "lethal levels of radiation and plague" (198). She is part of a woman-only community, all of whom are augmented "to endure, to survive, to hold our land" (198). In this description of Nili's home, Piercy extended the specific genre of feminist separatist utopias, such as Charlotte Perkins Gilman's *Herland* and Sally Miller Gearhart's *The Wanderground*. Although Nili's community is a highly technical and sophisticated society, they live isolated from the rest of the world as a security measure. Nili has come as "a spy and a scout" for her people, to explore and determine whether it is time to end their protective isolation (198).

A benefit of Riva's visit is the information she brings about Y-S and their long-term strategy, which involves a takeover of one of the other large multis (199). After extensive negotiations between Tikva and Y-S, a meeting is set. Riva and Nili will be present but invisible; Yod and Shira reject the originally agreed-to meeting point (inside Cybernaut, another multi) to insist that they meet outside any corporate control, in a tent where all sensors have been rendered inoperative. At the meeting, Y-S offers to reunite Shira with Josh and Ari, either on the Pacifica Platform where Josh and Ari now live or at the "Nebraska enclave" (217). Shira is also offered a promotion; she requests time to decide, which is denied. Shortly it becomes clear that accepting these offers is not intended to be optional. Shira is threatened: "Either you will agree to come with us, or you will come with us anyhow" (218). In the ensuing battle, Riva dies in an explosion, but Yod and Nili manage to kill the rest of the Y-S contingent before they escape back to Tikva.

Debriefing after the encounter, they all come to believe that Y-S has somehow learned about Yod and that the meeting was an excuse to try to take him; Y-S's Dr. Rhodes was avidly observing Yod throughout the meeting, paying no attention to the pretense of negotiating Shira's access to Ari. Malkah and Shira mourn Riva's death, although Shira's reactions are perplexing to her: "She could not properly mourn the woman she had never known, but neither could she pretend she had not just lost her biological mother" (223). She is confused by the complications of her emotional response. One might expect to grieve the death of any community member, but Shira feels something different at the death of her mother. Although she never knew Riva in a maternal role and, indeed, asserts to herself that "I am Malkah's daughter, not yours" (200), Shira still feels a loss.

As Y-S's pursuit of Shira becomes increasingly aggressive, Tikva responds by invading the Y-S Base. Their dual mission—to gain information and to insert worms and other viruses—is successful. In processing the information gathered, they discover that Avram and Yod "are the real targets of Y-S" (282). Somehow Y-S is cognizant of the nature of Avram's research and allowed Shira to return to Tikva to learn what that research had produced, with the intention of recalling her to Y-S and retrieving from her memory what she knows. In trying to determine their next steps, Malkah asks, "now that we know what they want, what do we want?" (282).

There are several different answers. Avram asserts, "we want our independence." Shira desires her son, and Yod wishes to "end the threat to this town. I want to be free then, free to live as I want and choose" (283). Avram scoffs at this but Shira and Malkah are supportive. Although the issue of Yod's status must be tabled in the face of the imminent threat from Y-S, at some point it will have to be addressed by the town. If he is a true member of the community, he is entitled to certain rights, including an "economic identity," which means he should be paid for his labor (212). Shira and Gadi are united in their support of Yod, although for different reasons. Shira wants her lover to be independent, with more ability to navigate outside Avram's control. Gadi acknowledges that he relishes "an opportunity to frustrate my father" (210), not a particularly admirable motive but one which serves to benefit Yod and Shira.

In the time of Joseph, violence also looms. It is almost Easter and the Maharal worries about "a time of pogroms" (204), sending Joseph into the city to attempt to learn what, if anything, is planned. He finds that, indeed, some of the townsmen are planning a riot (206). The Maharal employs diplomatic strategies to gain protection but he and Joseph also rally people to stand against Father Thaddeus, the leader of the mob which has come to kill Jews. After a huge street fight resulting in many dead and wounded, the invaders leave and the "battle of Good Friday is over" (347). Thaddeus switches targets and begins to agitate among the Protestants, a group more important to the Emperor's interests. When the Emperor takes steps to limit the effectiveness of Thaddeus and other inciters in response, it seems that the Jewish neighborhood is safe for now. Because of this, the Maharal decides that Joseph's usefulness has ended and he must be unmade. The men who helped the Maharal create Joseph are summoned, which leads to a conversation about Joseph's status, similar to conversations in Tikva about Yod's. One of the men is reluctant, arguing that Joseph "isn't human, but he thinks, he feels" (397). The Maharal is unconvinced, insisting that "I made him. I must unmake him" (398). The Maharal's statement echoes and foreshadows Avram's use of the exact same phrases later in the novel.

In Tikva, measures of resistance and defense are also being employed, including an attempt to recruit allies. Nili plans to go to the Glop, the place where "day workers and gang niños and the unemployed" live (31). Many are concerned because the Glop appears a lawless and dangerous place; Malkah notes, "the Glop is chaos" (285). But the chaos is useful to some as concealment. Riva had advised Nili to make contact with resistance forces in the Glop. Apparently Riva had been pirating information for self-governing groups in the Glop who are organizing against the multis. Gadi, Nili, Shira, and Yod travel together to see if there are any potential allies in these groups. Nili has been given coordinates to meet Lazarus, one of the resistance leaders.

In Christian mythology, Lazarus is someone who has been restored to life; his name offers a clue to an upcoming event. Upon their arrival at the resistance compound, Riva appears, seemingly resurrected from death to life. The Tikva contingent learns that Nili and Riva decided to fake her death at the Y-S meeting because Y-S was getting too close and she needed "more maneuvering room" (305). As when she previously faced Riva's death, Shira's emotions are "muddled" (304); she feels guilt, anger, and confusion. She is also furious that Malkah doesn't yet know that her own daughter is alive. Lazarus and his Coyotes are working to be less dependent on Y-S; they're building their own Net; working toward food self-sufficiency; educating and training their children; and organizing a union. They are finding ways to subvert corporate control and to assert their agency. Riva sees them as useful partners in her efforts.

Tikva's Council is also discussing responses to any attack by Y-S. The community trains for defense, building relationships with Lazarus and his people and negotiating with other multis for protection. Y-S instigates a confrontation by accusing Tikva of "harboring a murderer" (385); when Yod and Shira successfully infiltrated Y-S to retrieve Ari, Yod was forced to kill Josh in order to keep him from alerting security. At a meeting in the Net, high-level Y-S leaders demand that Yod be turned over to them, threatening "a program of incursions" on Tikva's Base if they do not accede to the demand (392). Y-S then preempts their own ultimatum by sending assassins prior to the deadline. They are quickly killed by Yod.

While waiting to experience any other consequences of their resistance to Y-S, Avram informs the town's Council of Yod's true identity. Gadi has told the Council that Yod is not being paid and others have noticed his constant presence and "put in a complaint of overwork on his behalf" (364). This raises an existential question. Will the Council "decide that Yod was a citizen of Tikva or Avram's tool" (366)? Shira is hopeful that Yod will be freed from Avram's control, while Yod begins to wrestle with the morality of his existence. He was "designed to be a weapon" (366), but he wants a life with Shira and her son.

As the Council meets to "rule whether Yod was the property of Avram or of the town, or whether he was a citizen" (403), Riva discovers that Y-S wants Yod at a high-level meeting and they learn that Avram has decided to send him to the meeting to "self-destruct" (407) and destroy as many Y-S workers as he can. Here is where Avram's response echoes the Maharal's. When challenged by Malkah, Shira, and others, Avram claims the power of creation and destruction, asserting that "I made him, and I can unmake him" (408). Yod is easily replaceable to him; Avram simply intends to build a new cyborg after Yod is destroyed. Shira is outraged. Yod is struggling with the injustice of his existence: "I don't want to be a conscious weapon. A weapon that's conscious is a contradiction, because it develops attachments, ethics, desires. It doesn't want to be a tool of destruction" (410).

While Malkah, Shira and Nili wait to hear the results of Yod's task, Malkah notes miserably that "you're the right path, Nili. It's better to make people into partial machines than to create machines that feel and yet are still controlled like cleaning robots. The creation of a conscious being as any kind of tool—supposed to exist only to fill our needs—is a disaster" (412). They hear an explosion; Avram, the lab, and his records are all destroyed. Listening to a message Yod has pre-recorded for Shira prior to his departure, she discovers that he has intentionally blown up the lab and killed Avram: "I want there to be no more weapons like me. A weapon should not be conscious. . . . I die knowing I destroy the capacity to replicate me" (415). If the humanized machine is not autonomous, its human characteristics interfere with its duties. If it is autonomous, human fears of being controlled by robots surface.

Shira grieves Yod's death as if she were his widow. She is appointed to Malkah's place as a Base Overseer and finds "in herself a swelling power, an intensifying concentrated energy for work" (423). When she discovers Avram's research logs in Malkah's office, it occurs to her momentarily that she could build "a mate . . . a Yod who belonged only to her" (425). Quickly she remembers Yod's act of destruction, his insistence that others like him should not be created. Tamping down her own sorrow and desire, Shira honors Yod's wishes by destroying the materials that contain the knowledge to create Yod's replacement. She feels that she "has set him free" (429).

Haraway has argued that "monsters have always defined the limits of community in Western imaginations" (180). Monsters are outside of community; those who are not monsters populate the community. Questions about who counts as a human being and who has status in a community run through both Yod's and Joseph's stories. The Maharal and Avram each see their creation as a tool, a weapon to be mobilized at their will, regardless of the desires of their creations. Yod and Joseph, however, live as though they are human, accepted by and integrated into their communities. Joseph has no control over the moment of his demise by the Maharal. Yod cannot resist his ultimate destruction as a result of Avram's decision, but can and does assert autonomy over the choice of that moment and of the conditions that follow. Avram and the Maharal are judged negatively by some because of their decision to destroy that which they created. Perhaps it is their behavior that is monstrous and outside the boundary of community. Shira thinks of Yod as "a person, although not a human one" (421), acknowledging a more inclusive understanding of personhood, if not humanness. Or, if we are all cyborgs, as Shira argued to Yod, then are we are all monsters too?

As Malcolm Bosse wrote in his *New York Times* review of the book, "Marge Piercy confronts large issues in this novel; the social consequences of creating anthropomorphic cyborgs, the dynamics of programming both humans and machines, the ethical question of our control of machines that might feel as well as think." These are questions that continue to be important in a time of rapidly developing technological capability that often exceeds our ability to understand its implications or to develop appropriate ethics in response.

CHAPTER FIVE

Fly Away Home and *The Longings of Women*
Home, Housing, and Homelessness

Piercy's novels *Fly Away Home* (1984) and *The Longings of Women* (1994) offer a sustained focus on issues of home, housing politics, and homelessness. Although homelessness can affect anyone, women are particularly at risk. This is due at least in part to the gendered wage gap, as well as to time spent at home and out of the paid workforce to care for children. These factors impact women's wages; long-term economic security; and their ability to support themselves and their families. Piercy's two novels tell the stories of women made vulnerable by their husbands' infidelities and their ultimate divorces, and by the significant consequences that result from a lack of economic independence.

In a review of *Longings* that is also an accurate description of Piercy's work in general, Elayne Rapping writes of "her special mix of juicy readability and social seriousness in treating the joys and traumas of contemporary American women's lives" (46). Both of these novels deal with significant social justice issues, but each one also asserts the value and the pleasures of creating a warm and nurturing home. In *The Longings of Women,* the intersecting stories of Leila, Becky, and Mary put a human face on "the homeless." As Leila develops some understanding of the situation of homeless and housing-insecure women, she begins to work for solutions. In *Fly Away Home,* Daria is faced with the destruction of her marriage and is confronted with the reality that her husband is a slumlord. While Daria fights to be treated fairly in her divorce, she joins an organization struggling for housing justice, taking action on her own behalf and for others. Both novels address the practices and consequences of gentrification.[1]

In 1963, Betty Friedan's *The Feminine Mystique* illuminated the realities of many American women. Friedan's discussion of the "problem that has no name" (15), which particularly afflicted the white, middle- to upper-class suburban housewife of the United States, galvanized a generation of women. The problem—dissatisfaction, guilt, boredom—could not be articulated by the women who experienced it but was internalized by them. Friedan wrote: "If a woman had a problem in the 1950's and 1960's, she knew that something must be wrong with her marriage, or with herself" (14). Friedan names the problem: a "lack of identity" (172), an absence of identity outside of the socially-sanctioned generic wife and mother. Friedan's book has been critiqued, and rightly so, for its avoidance of issues of class, race, and ethnicity. Megan Behrent commented that "working-class women and women of color, the majority of whom by necessity already worked outside of the home (often in the homes of other women) are entirely absent from Friedan's work."

Friedan also failed to exhibit any awareness of her own heteronormativity as she assumed that everyone is or should be heterosexual, a cultural expectation which would not have been unusual at the time.[2] It is apparent retrospectively that her generalizations apply to a limited group of women: educated, upper-middle class, heterosexual white women.[3] In the Epilogue to the tenth edition of *The Feminine Mystique,* Freidan describes some of her activism in the women's movement, acknowledging that "I never did see it in term of class or race" (270). Nevertheless, Friedan's explanations of the way the feminine mystique affected American culture helped to politicize thousands of women. As Behrent noted, "it destroyed the myth of the domestic bliss of the happy housewife," thus having an "ideological effect."

Sara Evans noted that "the feminine mystique of the 1950s had blinded American women to the realities of their experience" (213). An important question in Friedan's work centers on the issue of who gets to define reality and how certain versions of reality are enforced; she asks, "What force in our culture is strong enough to write 'Occupation: housewife' so large that all the other possibilities for women have been almost obscured?" (196). Friedan makes clear that for the women she is speaking to and about, reality was defined in large part by the mass media, the institution of Freudian psychoanalysis, and functionalist strains of social science; all of these constructed a normalizing vision of "woman" (115–16). Male privilege and the expectations and demands of fathers and husbands also played (and continue to play) a part in limiting women's choices and autonomy.

Carol Sternhell's review of *Fly Away Home* describes the book as "the absorbing story of a conventional suburban woman's personal and political awakening" (363). The protagonist, Daria Walker, is in many ways the woman Friedan describes in *The Feminine Mystique,* a woman molded by societal and familial expectations. Daria is married to Ross, a successful attorney, and they have two grown daughters. Theirs is a fairly stereotypical marriage: Ross has a career and controls the money (even Daria's income); Daria's focus is the house and she is given—or expected to assume—total responsibility for it, even as she juggles a successful and demanding career as a cookbook writer. And yet, Daria experiences significant pleasure in building a comfortable home, cooking delicious food, and creating her garden, taking great pride in all of this: "She had put enormous effort into house and garden, her treasure, her artwork, her outer skin" (18). Though some might see these as thankless chores, these activities do not seem limiting or burdensome to Daria.

But, reading *The Feminine Mystique* against *Fly Away Home,* it becomes clear that Daria is experiencing Friedan's identity crisis. Although she has a successful career, Daria cannot fully claim that identity. She gets a second phone line, because Ross doesn't want to be bothered taking messages for her. When Daria travels on business, she cooks and freezes meals ahead of time so Ross will not be inconvenienced. She spends time and psychic energy minimizing the impact her work has on their life as a couple and as a family. Daria is so successful at muffling her accomplishments, that her daughter Tracy is totally unaware of her celebrity status. On Tracy's first visit home from college, she says to Daria: "Some of the girls at school, they've heard of you. I mean, I never realized you're famous. I always thought your books were . . . kind of a family joke. But they've seen you on television" (13). Daria quickly changes the subject, feeling that "talking too much about her work or the modest measure of celebrity it had brought felt dangerous around the house, even if Ross wasn't in earshot" (14). In fact, Ross covers his jealousy of his wife's success with scorn, disparaging and minimizing her achievement, saying at one point: "I'm trying to achieve something. . . . Everyone created such a fuss, as if yours were any sort of real work. Taking something that every woman does as a matter of course and making a fetish of it" (370).

It is not only her inability to fully inhabit the identity of "successful cookbook writer" that is problematic for Daria. In some sense, she cannot see herself as separate from Ross. That she shares his name is confirmation for Daria of her identity: "For her whole adult life, her name had been Daria Walker" (68). This is also a sign of their inseparability: "Ross and Daria, Ross and Daria, that was who she was" (68). She questions, "without Ross, what did she have to show for her life?" (158).

Ross encourages Daria's muting, and even erasure, of a separate identity, demanding as his due her sublimation of herself into his life. Ross defines Daria's reality, constructing a vision of "wife" which suits him, and expecting her to occupy that space. In fact, he is unable to acknowledge any part of Daria that exists outside of his selective notions or that has the potential to create any discomfort in his world. His articulation of who she should be is so convincing that Daria has almost lost the ability to believe in what she knows to be real; and, when Daria's instincts or experiences do not match Ross's interpretation, she, along with her thoughts, feelings, and values, are degraded, criticized, or ignored. It takes outsiders to give Daria the capability to claim her own knowledge; the confidence to articulate her experience and own it; and the courage to see clearly. And no wonder—Friedan asked: "How can any woman see the whole truth within the bounds of her own life? How can she believe that voice inside herself, when it denies the conventional, accepted truths by which she has been living?" (26).

Daria's oldest daughter, Robin, models herself on her father, echoing Ross's devaluation of Daria, her work and her interests. Daria sees Robin as someone who is "hotly ambitious and seemed to believe that she would be rich and what she considered a success in a matter of a few years" (73). Robin was strongly competitive in high school and college, and "needed intensely to win" (112). Ross and Robin jog together in the city most mornings before work; they watch football together after Saturday lunch; Robin seems "spirited" with Ross (73) in ways she doesn't with Daria. Robin will barely eat meals Daria has cooked, and is on a constant diet which, Robin says, is just "a matter of willpower" (72). Daria makes sense of the distance Robin imposes in their relationship by thinking, "all children prefer one parent over the other" (112). And, indeed, Daria does have a closer relationship with her younger daughter, feeling that "Tracy needed her, whereas Robin didn't seem to need anyone, or wouldn't admit it if she did" (7). Daria also finds Tracy more similar to her, since Tracy takes "after her in appearance, in emotional temperature, in sensual nature" (7). Paralleling the relationship between Robin and Daria, Tracy is often at odds with Ross and feels judged by him: "It's my way he can't stand. It's me" (9).

A catalyzing moment for Daria occurs when she discovers that Ross is a slum landlord involved in hiring arsonists to torch buildings in areas slated for gentrification. Daria is unknowingly listed as the owner of some of these buildings, as Ross manipulates trusts, corporate affiliations, and multiple ownerships in a maze of impossible-to-trace paperwork. She is accustomed to being asked to sign various papers without having them explained to her or asking about them. Daria is confronted with the situation Ross has created when a group of activists from the targeted area arrive to picket in front of her house. The Save Our Neighborhood (SON) members are distrustful of her ignorance, feeling that it is disingenuous and self-serving. How could she not know about buildings she owns or her husband's activities? SON members also resent Daria's class privilege, a privilege which is in some ways invisible to her. One of the activists, Tom, points this out to her: "You've made a big decision to be innocent. Totally innocent. What kind of luxury is that?" (139). She has the privilege not to know what is going on at the property she legally owns, but it is a privilege that leaves her vulnerable.

When Daria's marriage implodes, Ross moves out. She discovers that he has been having an affair with a younger woman, Gail, who he quickly marries once their divorce is final and who becomes pregnant (it is not clear to Daria whether Gail is pregnant when she and Ross marry). After consulting an attorney, she realizes that she is dangerously uninformed about their finances and that she is deeply implicated in Ross's business dealings, whatever they are. He assumes that she will simply accept whatever divorce settlement he offers, but Daria is determined to have an equitable one. A SON member, Sandra Maria, teaches her how to search title records and ascertain property ownership. This information is vital to Daria for getting a fair settlement in her divorce, but it is also useful for SON, as they try to hold someone accountable for the attempts to destroy their neighborhood. As Daria begins to contribute more of her time to SON and their work, she and Tom become intimately involved. It is a very different relationship for Daria than her marriage. She is able to be more herself with him and she feels that they are more honest with each other. Tom values her as a mature, professional, competent, and creative woman, which helps Daria begin to realize that "never with Ross had she felt equal" (353).

When Daria initially recognizes that her marriage is falling apart, she is shocked to discover that Robin is fully informed about Ross's affair. Again Robin has aligned herself with Ross and his perspective, blaming their estrangement on Daria: "It's your fault, Mother. You don't appreciate him. He's got to grow and change and everything, just like me" (106). When Daria discloses the status of her marriage to Tracy before Tracy is due to come home for the holidays, Tracy is harshly judgmental of her sister's allegiance to Ross, exclaiming, "Robin is a suck and a wimp" (130).

After a few hours of peace when the family comes together on Christmas Eve, Robin and Tracy begin an argument during which it becomes apparent that Ross has shared with Robin a version of their marriage not grounded in reality; Robin believes that Daria "made him marry you" because she was pregnant (154). In fact, Daria had planned to have an abortion until Ross convinced her to marry and begin their family. Robin attaches to this revisionist history as a way to stay loyal to her father at the expense of her relationship with Daria. It's not until after Ross remarries that Robin reconnects with Daria. Absorbed in his new relationship, he has no time for Robin and she feels abandoned: "I tried so hard to please him!" (346). Daria feels sympathy for Robin, but is not willing to spend much time thinking about Ross: "What you have to figure out with me is not how to get close to your father again, because that's none of my business. What you must work out with me is how to be closer to me. How we can love each other" (348).

As Daria and Robin become reconciled, Tom is also working out his relationships with her daughters. Although Tracy's sympathies have consistently remained with her mother, she is nonetheless a little surprised, although not unpleasantly so, to find Daria in a relationship with Tom. Tracy warms to him quickly, but Robin is a little more hesitant, eventually finding points of connection over sports and games. When Tom's daughters, who are younger than Daria's, visit from the West Coast, Daria begins to get to know them as well. Both Tom and Daria work to build connections with each other's children, engaging with them as people, not just as family members of a new partner.

The relationship between Tom and Daria is also embedded in the community in which they are enmeshed, although Tracy observes that Daria is the nexus around which activity revolves. Robin shares Tracy's conclusions with Daria: "She says it's really a women's house. A strong women's house. And that everybody likes that. That's why so many people hang around" (397). These relational configurations transcend the model of the blood-related nuclear family in a way that gestures to the limitations of the nuclear family in contributing to society and meeting the needs of its members.

For some time, Daria remains unconvinced that the conclusions SON is drawing about the neighborhood buildings burning down can be accurate. SON members are convinced these fires have been caused by arson, planned intentionally to assist Ross and his partners' gentrification efforts. Although she is angry at Ross and, in fact, realizes that she has come to dislike him intensely, she can't believe he is a criminal or would be so callous and unfeeling as to put people's lives at risk. Tom is annoyed by her continuing reluctance to understand what is going on: "You want to be blind . . . That's the thing I resent most about you. You think there's virtue in pretending not to notice" (243). Daria's sister Gussie also accuses her of liking to "play dumb. . . . You pretend you don't catch on to things you don't want to notice" (194–95). Daria has indeed unconsciously taken advantage of the privilege of being unaware. Critics, too, have noted Daria's naiveté. John Clute described "her incapacity to understand the world" as "near-lunacy" (658). Jeanne McManus pointed out that it is only when Ross is "too terribly villainous to ignore" that Daria is forced to recognize who and what her husband has become.

In her book *Feminism and Its Fictions,* Lisa Maria Hogeland summed up the response of many male reviewers to feminist novels of the 1970s and 1980s that are "perceived to impinge on, to set limits to, or to critique men's behavior" as: "men can't be that bad" (84). Some reviews of *Fly Away Home* proceed in this vein. Clute described Ross as someone we must notice is "a ruthless male chauvinist, an adulterer, a liberal turned very conservative indeed, a shyster lawyer, and a jogger, but also that he is deeply involved in murder and arson." For Clute, Piercy's characterization of Ross is a "great flaw" in the novel—as a character, Ross more properly belongs in "genre fiction" (658). It's not clear why the fact that Ross is a jogger is a relevant factor in Clute's argument but, despite his condemnation of Piercy's portrayal of Ross, Clute ended his review with a positive assessment of the novel. Overall Clute identified *Fly Away Home* as a novel that leaves readers "with a sense of engagement with the decency of human lives"—the "heart" of the book.

Female critics have also taken exception to the ways in which Piercy created Ross's character. Elizabeth Wheeler described him as "cardboard," with "the charm of bubble gum on the bottom of a shoe," noting that Daria is "the only complete character in the book." She also commented on the impact of "estrangement in a long marriage," as a demonstration of how people can grow apart. Jane O'Reilly observes that the novel doesn't explain "how Ross has become a grandiose megalomaniac" (7). McManus, who calls Daria "often simple-minded" and "too naïve," suggested that Daria's experience of living "22 years with a man who turns out to have lied, to have deceived, to have burned out the woman's trust to the core" will be familiar to other women who have had similar experiences. Indeed, sometimes this is exactly how bullies operate: they can be both superficially charming and also domineering, as they mask their exercise of power and control with smoothness. When one's own life is dependent upon the reactions and responses of another person, it can be difficult to ascertain the truth for oneself. And, who wants to believe that their life has been built on manipulation?[4] Still, it seems that on balance, despite these criticisms of Daria's misguided willingness to believe for far too long in the basic decency of her husband, and of Ross being an extremely one-dimensional character, these critics find the novel's plot relatable and convincing.

When Daria's own house is burnt down, she has to come to terms with the fact that "in the person of Ross whom she had loved she had encountered evil" (286). Accepting this reality is what allows Daria finally to throw off Ross's mystification and control of her life. Claiming autonomy and recognizing her abilities is what enables Daria to negotiate her way through a divorce successfully; to begin to build a new life; and, ultimately, to join the fight for social justice, allying with SON to achieve safe and affordable housing for everyone. Daria sees that her personal experiences are connected to the political. Those experiences are enmeshed in broad societal power asymmetries and the two cannot be separated—a connection that second-wave feminism pointedly acknowledged in its slogan: "The personal is the political." Barbara Andolsen argues that "we cannot accept rifts between knowing and doing or among separated areas of life. What happens in the kitchen or the bedroom is significant for what happens in boardrooms and on city streets" (xx).

Piercy has mined this patriarchally-enforced separation between the public and private, where the equation of women with private space and domesticity and the consequent devaluing of this space has continuing and deep economic consequences for women. Piercy's protagonist identifies very strongly with domesticity. Daria's house is part of her identity; tending to it signifies love and caring and stability and security for her. Her career is established in a domestic sphere—she writes cookbooks. And her eventual activism is related to access to safe and healthy places to live. But Daria's identification with her home and her refusal to lose it also sets the battle lines for her resistance to Ross's inadequate divorce settlement offers. Later, the economic benefits of her career allow her to create a new home where she can rediscover her strengths; reclaim her knowledge; build new relationships and a new community; and create and inhabit her own reality.

Susan Mernit described Daria as someone "who wants to create fair, comfortable, conditions for everybody and who finds other people to help her do it" (18). Her activism focuses on the politics of housing in a wide social context, asserting the centrality and importance of adequate housing for everyone. In this way, Piercy has refused the oversimplified contempt for matters of the home. Daria doesn't have to transcend the space of domesticity to become her own person; and, through her, the reader comes to understand differently the power of domesticity and the strategies by which its values can infuse action and activities outside of the home. As readers, we might ask a variety of questions about this. Does the attraction of the domestic focus solely on the home and private space and, if so, is that experienced as problematic or limiting? If yes, are those limitations imposed by the values and expectations of others? Do we benefit from a clear separation of private and public space, or is it possible for the ethos of domesticity to impact lives in arenas outside the home in productive and generative ways? Piercy has offered a range of responses to those questions.

Daria moves through a process of empowering herself to act in a variety of ways. Andolsen described a set of possible responses to injustice this way: "Telling our stories to each other and making judgments about injustice and justice leads women into action. Such actions may be as simple as helping another woman to see what options she has tomorrow. Or they may be as complex and long range as commitments and actions to change the balance of political power between the sexes or to revamp the economic system" (xvii). Daria's political actions occur at these multiple levels. On a personal level, she works out a communal living arrangement that assists activist Sandra Maria and her daughter Mariela when they are burned out of their home. On a more global level, her fight for and commitment to safe and affordable housing in the neighborhood acts as an intervention which disrupts gentrification projects, affecting housing politics on a city-wide level. The personal is the political; and, understanding the politicization of the personal is a crucial step toward enabling change, one which creates the ability to define one's own reality and critically examine the forces which are invested in mystifying it.

Piercy's interest in the politics of housing and domesticity continues in *The Longings of Women*. The novel is told through the perspectives of three women whose stories and lives intersect: Leila Landsman, Becky Burgess, and Mary Burke. In some ways, the main protagonist, Leila, is very similar to Daria. She has a successful career as a sociology professor who also writes books on topics of interest to the general public, and she also arranges her life to accommodate the needs of her husband, Nick, a well-known regional theater director. Her house is important to her, too, serving as a place of comfort and retreat. Nick's infidelities are an ongoing accompaniment to their marriage. This was part of the original agreement—that Nick would retain his freedom, that he had tacit permission to be unfaithful. Although Leila puts on the façade of acceptance of the arrangement, she is angry and resentful. She struggles to suppress these feelings so as not to jeopardize her marriage, trying to rationalize her choice: "To any relationship there were costs, there were imposed overt and hidden taxes" (7).

Leila is asked by her publisher to write a book about the Becky Burgess case. Burgess is accused of conspiring with her younger lover to kill her husband.[5] Initially reluctant, Leila agrees, in part because "The money's good, very good" (19), an important motivator as she is the main wage-earner in the family. Becky is one of several children from a poor family in New Bedford—and although she loves her family, she is determined to escape poverty, deprivation and worry. "She wasn't going to hang around the way everybody else in her family just seemed rooted in the sand of their yard" (26). Becky wanted money, success, and quality possessions: "She never gave up studying How Things Should Be" (128) so she could build the life she wanted. The first in her family to attend college, she worked her way through a four-year degree, seeking a career in television. Taking an office job at a cable company after graduation, she hopes to navigate her way into an on-camera position. Becky is strategic, manipulative, and focused. When she encounters computer technician Terry Burgess at the company, she sees him as her way out, as "the perfect walking embodiment of all she longed for" (154). Terry's family is well-ensconced in a comfortable, middle-class existence; his mother, in particular, clearly disapproves of Becky because of her background and family's economic status (similar to Murray's family's reaction to Ruthie in *Gone to Soldiers*). When Terry's mother pressures him to replace Becky with a new girlfriend, he is furious. Becky is quick to take advantage of his anger with his mother and suggests marriage. The couple lives first in an apartment, and then Terry's parents help them buy a condominium.

Tension quickly emerges in their marriage. Encouraged by a neighbor, Becky begins to spend her evenings acting in a community theater, where she meets Sam, a high-school student who is infatuated with her. Terry loses his job and seems unable to get another—although he is clearly not working very hard to find one—so Becky is supporting the household. As their relationship deteriorates, Terry starts to talk about divorce, noting their class differences as a point of incompatibility. Becky discovers he is having an affair and, most disturbingly to her, is in the process of changing the beneficiary on his life insurance policy away from Becky to his mother. This galvanizes Becky—she pretends to be interested in making their marriage better as a way to "buy herself some time to think, to figure things out" (298). However, she also finds Sam's interest in her flattering and begins an affair with him. Eventually Becky decides to leverage their sexual relationship to convince Sam to kill Terry. This solution, melodramatic and desperate though it seems, feels to Becky like her only choice to retain her tenuous hold on a middle-class existence.

The novel gives the reader Becky's experiences in her own voice and perspective in parallel with the information Leila learns in researching the case. Leila watches old news footage and interviews people who knew Becky, Terry, and Sam, eventually talking directly with Becky and Sam. It is clear that Becky's single-focused ambition, to move out of poverty and have an economically comfortable and secure life, drives all of her actions. In any encounter, she is sharply observant, adopting whatever attitudes and actions she believes will help her to succeed.

Also struggling to survive is Mary Burke, divorced after a twenty-plus year marriage to an upper-middle class man. At the time of her divorce, Mary received a less-than-equitable settlement. Hogeland went so far as to describe *Longings* as an "overtly political novel about women's impoverishment after divorce" (169). Mary initially makes ends meet by working a low-income job at a stationery store near the small apartment she has rented, but Boston University claims both her apartment building and the store in which she works in order to build student housing (277). Unable to afford a new place, Mary ends up homeless; "Before she had been evicted, it had become evident she could afford nothing that existed, and the wait for public housing was forever and a day" (277). Mary feels unable to tell anyone, even her children, of her predicament. Her fear of people's reactions to her lack of housing seems quite accurate: "She could not let any of her clients find out she was homeless, for she would be out of a job in nothing flat. Nobody would want her in their houses; nobody would trust her. She heard people talking about the homeless, how they were crazy, they were drug addicts, they didn't want to work. How unpleasant it was to be panhandled, how they should be kept off the streets. How pitiful and dirty they were. As if there weren't thousands like her who worked every day without making enough for a deposit and rent" (17). Piercy's poem "Woman in the Bushes" in *Mars and Her Children* offers a description of a situation like Mary's: "Her only house her back bearing / All the clothing remaining to her" (5–6).

Although Mary has no home, she finds another job, working through a cleaning service. Leila Landsman is one of her clients. Because of the information Mary has access to in cleaning the Landsman house, she is aware of Nick's infidelities. She compares Leila's situation with her own. When Mary, at forty-five, found out her husband had been sleeping with his secretary, they divorced. Mary feels that she must have "far more pride than Mrs. Landsman, because she wouldn't take his crap. . . . She had been a good wife and a good mother, and she was entitled to a good husband" (82). Mary's justifiable unwillingness to swallow her pride makes her economically vulnerable, and eventually lands her on the streets. Mary knows the price Leila pays to accommodate her husband and the price Mary herself paid when she left: "Mrs. L. put up with a lot to stay married. How could Mary judge her harshly, considering what divorce meant to an older woman? Here she was, walking evidence, exhibit number one" (38). Although Mary's job provides some income, it does little to increase her housing options since her wages are insufficient to accumulate the deposit necessary for an apartment and utilities.

Piercy's descriptions of Mary's life on the streets demonstrate how difficult the details of daily life become without a home. How does one keep clean? Where does one sleep? What can one eat with little money and no stove or refrigerator? Where is there access to a bathroom? As Mary observes, "Nothing you really needed to do when you were homeless was supposed to happen. You were illegal" (310). Society blames homeless people for being homeless, and then blames them again when they do what they must to survive.[6]

That is one significant difference in their situations: Leila has some economic security through her job, her books, and her speaking engagements, and thus more options when her marriage ends. While she gathers the material for her book, Leila discovers that Nick is having an affair with Sheryl, the star of the play he is directing in New York, and she then learns Sheryl is pregnant. In coming to terms with this development, she realizes that she is no longer willing to compromise or tolerate Nick's actions: "Her husband having a baby with a young woman was not a situation she was prepared to ignore" (224). For her, this is the end of the marriage. Although the chronology, circumstances, and context of Nick and Leila's divorce differ from that of Ross and Daria's, the situations are in some ways similar: a philandering husband, a younger woman, an impending baby, and a contentious divorce. Resisting pressure from Nick, she refuses to sell their house hastily and take a loss. When their son, David, expresses concern about how she will manage financially post-divorce, she is astonished: "Is it possible you don't know I've basically supported the household for the past ten years?" (252). After the divorce, Leila buys her own home, deciding to pay it off as quickly as possible, despite her accountant's advice to continue to use it as a tax deduction. Moving money around on paper was not as important as a secure home. Mary affirms this priority as she muses on the advice she was given as a young girl: "Marry a professional man, they told her when she was growing up; they should have said, be a caterer, buy a property and pay it off fast. Never mind the rest. Get a job around food and a roof over your head that belongs to you and you alone" (276).

Mary's identity as a homeless woman makes her sensitive to the plight of other women living on the streets. She always speaks to a woman named Beverly when she sees her on the street, as a way to acknowledge their shared humanity. Later Beverly is raped and beaten, which prompts Mary to articulate a painful recognition of her own situation: "It was foolish to pretend that anything that happened to Beverly Bozeman could not happen to her" (183). She is vulnerable physically, as well as economically.

A fire in an abandoned building where Mary has been squatting leads to the death of three homeless people. Mary, ill and without other resources, must resentfully and reluctantly rely on Leila for shelter and assistance. As a result of this more intimate relationship, and after helping to provide Mary with at least a temporary solution to her housing problem by sending her to live with Leila's sister, Leila begins to write and speak on the subject of homeless women. She begins working with friends on "a range of projects involving homeless women" (426), including working to establish a house "where a group of women, aged twenty-seven to sixty-nine, were beginning to live together" (426). Mary is somewhat incredulous at Leila's new specialization, asking herself "What did Mrs. Landsman know about being homeless? . . . Had spending a week with her made Mrs. Landsman an expert on women without housing?" (425). The exposure had made Leila recognize how tenuous housing security is for any woman, including herself. Leila thinks: "There was nothing in the world like dealing with the homeless to make a woman engage in financial planning. It might not work, for there was no avoiding catastrophes, but meeting former housewives, teachers, factory workers, waitresses, secretaries made

Leila understand how fragile were the underpinnings of security for women. A man left or died, a job ended, a factory closed, a fire burned out her building, and she was out of money and on the streets" (427–28).

Throughout the novel, Piercy has forced her readers to recognize how vulnerable every woman is to homelessness. When Leila compares herself to Mary and the other homeless women she is working with, she recognizes how fragile economic security is. But even among the homeless, there are gradations of privilege. For example, when Mary compares herself to Beverly, she realizes the benefits inherent in being able to "pass" (279) as someone with housing, as she can. Still, "any woman could end up on the streets," Mary says (184), regardless of her actions. And Mary remains quite conscious of the potentially temporary nature of her situation with Leila's sister, reflecting that, "life has changed for me, but it could change back" (426). Access to economic security is unreliable at best.

Mary's lack of access to housing is an important aspect of the novel's development and momentum. Piercy also discusses the option of homeless shelters. Why doesn't Mary take refuge in a shelter? As readers we learn that shelters are not always safe; shelter space is only available for the night, so people have no place to go during the day; and the attitudes of shelter workers are often offensive to homeless people—either because of interactions dripping with pity or where shelter residents are treated with contempt or disdain. The novel does not posit long-term solutions and does not suggest public policy changes. The most intense focus is on providing services and shelter—finding a place for Mary and creating, as Leila is working to do, at least one house where some women can live. As Leila thinks about her activism and advocacy on behalf of homeless women, she observes that: "It was a matter not only of studying them, as other academics were doing [and an approach Mary criticizes], but of working to provide options, openings. She wanted as many choices as she could have, and she wanted those women to have choices too" (432).

These are not insignificant accomplishments, and they take a tremendous amount of commitment, effort, and creativity. But, ultimately, they are solutions that will be ineffective in solving the problems that create homelessness and housing insecurity. The novel promotes individual action and solidarity, but not necessarily the more pervasive or broad collective engagement that is called for. And, Mary's history makes clear that security achieved through individual decisions and actions is quite unreliable. It doesn't matter if you do the "right" thing—if you're a good wife, a good homemaker, a good worker—you are still vulnerable.

Still, the novel makes a significant contribution in challenging stereotypical images of homeless populations and humanizing faceless masses. In *The*

Longings of Women, the reader is not asked to look at "the homeless" but at Mary, and at the multiple factors that contribute to her homelessness. She is not homeless because of lack of effort, or some character flaw, and she exhibits incredible resilience and creativity in the face of her societally-endorsed marginalization.[7] This helps to develop a more accurate understanding of the life experiences of homeless populations, particularly of women, which can have an impact on housing policies. The novel helps to make "obvious to people what had been invisible to them before" (62). This can create attitudinal shifts that can help reduce the stigma attached to homeless people; force recognition of the societal processes that create homelessness; and increase support for the provision of affordable housing and economic justice. It's a shift that moves us beyond sympathy, pity, and charity—and toward an approach rooted in social justice and human rights.

CHAPTER 6

The Poetics of Piercy

Although Piercy's poetry is as sharply political as her novels, she also explores her family history and Jewish heritage; reproduction, mothers, and women's bodies; relationships—intimate, sexual, familial, friend; the cycles of nature; life on Cape Cod; the epiphanies that come from gardening and cats; and what her life as a writer is like. Many interviewers have asked Piercy about the process of writing poems and of writing novels and about whether she likes writing in one genre better than the other. Piercy discloses that "I would probably write poems in any circumstances" ("Interview with Karla Hammond" 25).

One of the distinctions she has made between poetry and fiction is this: "The heart of fiction is telling. The heart of poetry is utterance" (26). Fiction is a narrative, a movement through time, a story about "what happened next" (26). Poetry is about multiple ways of knowing "rational knowing . . . images . . . rhythms . . . sensual memories" (26). For Piercy, the process of writing poetry is "more intense, more concentrated," where a novel is "a microcosm. It is a little world I create, live in, and depart" ("An Interview with Peggy Friedman" 131). One of the ways Piercy has distinguished between poetry and fiction is that "poetry comes directly out of my life and the lives of those people around me, while fiction is about other people's lives" (Lyons 333). For her, "a novel is a far more artificial construction, and it takes huge amounts of time to write one" (333). Her motivation for writing fiction is "the desire to understand people and their choices through time. . . . Immersing myself in other lives satisfies me" (*Sleeping* 82). Although she enjoys writing both poetry and fiction (*Sleeping* 82), Piercy "could imagine not writing another novel; I couldn't imagine not writing poetry" (Lyons 333).

It would be difficult not to read many of her poems through the lens of her biography but, unlike some other poets for whom the "I" of the poem is a character they have constructed, Piercy has acknowledged that "usually the voice of the poems is mine" ("Circles" 18) and "in my poems I speak mostly in my own persona or in a voice that's a public form of it" ("Active" 92). Further, she acknowledged: "I write out of my own concerns, my ideas, my politics, my life, my curiosity, my pain and hunger and joy" (Hamner and Walker 150). Her poems, however, are not transparent, unmediated reflections of her life. Edith Wynne noted that "Piercy speaks directly to her readers in her own voice although she reminds us that the experiences she recounts are not always her own, nor are the poems confessional." Piercy added: "I believe that in my poems I am creating artifacts that speak for the experience of many people besides myself" (150).

Following the theme of being of use that pervades her work, Piercy shared that she has "always desired that my poems work for others. . . . What I mean by useful is simply that readers will find poems that speak to and for them . . . that the poems may give voice to something in the experience of a life" ("Circles" 19).[1] Piercy noted that she has readers who appreciate some of the themes of her poems and not others, but for her "it is all one vision" ("Circles" 22).

As with some of her comments on fiction, Piercy has overtly addressed the misconception that poetry is not political. She argues that "the notion that poetry with a conscious rather than an unconscious politics is impermissible or impure is a modern heresy of advantage only to those who like just fine the way things are going" ("Circles" 19). Piercy states that "attitude is itself political. Art which embodies the ideals of the ruling class in society isn't conceived of as being political, and is simply judged by how well it is done. Art which contains ideas which threaten the position of that ruling class is silenced by critics: it is political, they say, and not art. . . . It's absurd" ("Shaping Our Choices" 46). Thus, all art and cultural production is political; it is only a matter of whether readers choose to identify or ignore the politics embedded in the work.

Piercy's blog posts also interrupt the artificiality of lines between politics and art, as well as other oft-separated areas. For example, in her April 16, 2017 post, "A Good Seder," Piercy wrote: "I've begun thinking about the panel I'll be on in New York the first week in May. I have more thinking to do before I can start writing my speech. I wrote three new poems. We planted beets, Swiss chard, bullsblood, garden cress, leeks, arugula, dill, parsnips and put out calendula, pansies, fennel and parsley plants I'd started."[2] Here she ties an upcoming panel on "Gender, Power, and Authoritarianism in the Dystopian Age" (May 4, 2017 in New York City), with her current writing projects, and the state of her garden. This blending implies that, for Piercy, writing, gardening and contributing to a political panel all carry equal status and are of equal importance.

Piercy's early collection, *To Be of Use* (1969), is dedicated in part to women in the feminist movement and the mutual support that enables them to challenge restrictive societal norms and practices. Two of the sections are titled after individual poems within each section—"A Just Anger" and "The Spring Offensive of the Snail"—while the final section, "Laying Down the Tower," contains eleven poems representing the cards of a Tarot card reading. In the introduction to that section, Piercy notes that "this reading is political: the values are different than in more conventional ways of reading the deck" (71). In Piercy's reading of the Tarot cards she has chosen, she challenges and re-visions patriarchal values, symbols, and inherited myths. The collection's title, *To Be of Use,* reminds us that this desire to be of use also surfaces in several of her novels. Fred Moramarco and William Sullivan speak to this in their analysis of her work: "Though that work is diverse and reflects different stages of her life, it is important to her that poetry be *useful,* particularly to other women who will recognize themselves in various aspects of her life journey."

Other political issues, such as Piercy's interest in reproduction and issues of reproductive justice, run throughout her poetry. "Right to life,"[3] one of the poems in The Lunar Cycle section of *The Moon Is Always Female,* represents Saille, a month in the lunar calendar. In this poem, Piercy turns her attention to reproductive control and the unfortunately often-successful attempts to legislate restrictions on abortion. The poem is a direct address to the "you" who would attempt to control women's bodies in these ways. The poem argues that,

> A woman is not a pear tree
> thrusting her fruit in mindless fecundity
> into the world.
> . . . .
> A woman is not a basket you place
> your buns in to keep them warm. (1–3; 10–11)

It then sarcastically points out the hypocrisy of those who construct purportedly moral arguments to restrict or ban abortion:

> You value children so dearly
> that none ever go hungry, none weep
> with no one to tend them when mothers
> work, none lack fresh fruit,
> none chew lead or cough to death and your
> orphanages are empty. Every noon the best
> restaurants serve poor children steaks. (31–36)

The poem ends with an uncompromising assertion of female bodily integrity:

> I will choose what enters me, what becomes
> flesh of my flesh.
> . . . .
> You may not use me as your factory.
> . . . .
> This is my body. If I give it to you
> I want it back. My life
> is a non-negotiable demand. (58–59, 63, 66–68)

In the poem "Ethics for Republicans" (69),[4] from *Made in Detroit* and quoted here in full, Piercy attends to this same issue:

> An embryo is precious;
> a woman is a vessel.
>
> A fertilized egg is a person;
> a woman is indentured to it.
>
> An embryo is sacred until birth.
> After that, he/she is on their own.
>
> Abortion is murder. Rape,
> incest are means to an end:
>
> That precious fertilized egg
> housed in an expendable body.
>
> Let us make babies and babies
> and babies; children are something
>
> else, probably future criminals,
> probably welfare cheats whose
>
> education hikes taxes. You
> can freely dispose of them.

Here Piercy addresses the unconscionable attempts to enshrine into law the value of a fertilized egg over a woman's life through legislation that limits access to and/or attempts to criminalize abortion. Again, she calls out the hypocrisy of those who claim the sanctity of the life of an embryo, but refuse to protect and nurture the children who are born when they refuse to provide adequate funding for education and the social services which would provide a minimal safety net to enable children's growth and development. In an essay published a few years after the publication of *Made in Detroit,* Piercy has spoken of the tenuousness of the right of abortion and other reproductive issues: "With great effort we won the right of choice: to have a baby when we want one, access to safe contraception to prevent unwanted pregnancies, and the right to legal and safe abortion when we can't or don't want to take that on. Yet every month, those rights are slipping away in state legislatures and are now under siege by the federal government and Congress" ("Marge Piercy's 'Barbie Doll'"). As a consequence of the 2016 Presidential election, Piercy predicted, "I see the deaths of women from self-administered abortions and back alley abortions returning and the suffering to women and their families that caused" ("Despair").

The poem "A Just Anger" highlights the power of anger in the service of justice, alluding to the pressures put upon women to hide, deny, or mask their anger, and the consequences of that suppression. Piercy here used the technique of doubled or repeating lines to increase the strength and impact of her words. She emphasizes her anger, which moves from rage to the power of transformation. In this poem, which reads as deeply personal, Piercy has claimed the right to harness and use her anger. Johnette Rodriguez spoke to the galvanizing power of Piercy's poetry when she wrote: "Her poems were like banners for the movement, proclaiming pride in being a woman, rage at being the targets of man-made laws and man-made attitudes, and a fierce determination to effect change, both personal and political."

A different form of anger is seen in "The Wrong Anger" from *The Moon Is Always Female* (1977), a later collection. This poem makes visible the destructiveness of misplaced anger, when activists feel impotent and turn their frustration on each other. It points out the shallow satisfaction that attends this acting out of anger, yet notes that aiming anger at those with power is difficult. This poem notes that turning our anger against our allies is pointless and ultimately does nothing to interrupt the machinations of those in power and the impact of their decisions on other people.

"The Low Road," also from *The Moon Is Always Female,* is a very clear example of the way Piercy attends to issues of political power and empowerment in her poetry. The poem begins with an indictment of the many ways institutions in this country—government, military, corporations, medicine—have asserted and deployed power and control over individuals. It then focuses on the individual who confronts this overwhelming power and the strategies one person can employ to resist, which will all ultimately be unsuccessful. The poem then turns immediately from that moment of despair and helplessness to the beginning of possibility once the fight includes more than just one person. The poem moves on to cite the empowering capabilities and the path to positive results that come with joining with others and building coalitions. In addition to suggesting the need for and ways to struggle, the poem includes moments of pleasure, happiness, and joy. This poem sends a clear message about the importance and necessity of collective resistance to an unfair societal structure where institutions have more power than the people they allegedly serve.

The importance of the collective is revisited in "Hope is a Long, Slow Thing" from *Made in Detroit* (2015), which described disillusioned activists who do not see immediate results to their actions and then give up. In stanzas of three lines, the poem notes that all our struggles are important. Piercy traces the improvements that have been made as a result of the struggle as she looks back at her maternal family history. Her ancestors experienced death and poverty as they encountered world wars, the lack of ability to control reproduction, and sexual harassment. The poem ends with an encouraging message, noting that the only thing that has changed the world is the effort of those struggling for change and doing the work. Piercy herself is one of the staunch fighters and activists.

One of the political projects in which Piercy is currently active is the effort to close the Pilgrim Nuclear Power Station in Plymouth. In the event of a nuclear incident, few—if any—people on Cape Cod would be able to evacuate safely due to the inadequate road infrastructure and limited ingress/egress to the peninsula. In "One of the Expendables," also from *Made in Detroit,* Piercy reflected on living in the vicinity of a nuclear power plant and refers to the 2011 nuclear disaster in Japan. After describing the decades-long consequences of nuclear contamination to the environment, and calling out the lack of options residents and tourists on the Cape face, Piercy criticizes the corporations who care more about their profits than people's lives.

Again and again in Piercy's poems, we are confronted with the impunity of corporations and institutions which demonstrate no awareness of the consequences of their actions and decisions, and which are not held accountable in any way. On April 14, 2016, David Abel and John R. Ellement's article in the *Boston Globe,* "Closing Date Set for Pilgrim Nuclear Power Plant," discussed the significant environmental and health concerns at the plant and noted that it is currently scheduled to be decommissioned in 2019. In February 2017, Piercy wrote: "At the same time, the NRC[5] is refusing to close Pilgrim nuclear power plant in spite of their own reports on its lax security and dreadful problems in upkeep, repair and accidents. They are insisting on refueling it in spite of huge protests here. Now there are rumros [*sic*] about Entergy selling the plant to someone who will continue to run it" ("I'm Better as the World Crashes").

Other poems observe attempts to control women through focusing on women's appearance and behavior, issues that second-wave feminism understood as the politics of beauty and societal expectations of femininity. In "A Work of Artifice" from *To Be of Use,* Piercy employed the metaphor of the bonsai tree to make visible the rigid limitations of acceptability within which women must operate. Using the metaphor of the pruned bonsai tree, Piercy made visible all the ways in which society tells women to stay small and contained, to make sure their energy goes into meeting conventional standards of attractiveness—whatever those might be in any given society at any given time.

This same crippling, even deadly, conformity is exposed in the poem "Barbie Doll," from *To Be of Use,* which is an excellent example of Piercy's attention to these issues. She shared her motivation for writing the poem: "This poem is written to show how from the day little girls are born they are subjected to their gender role. It goes on to talk about how the what was on the inside didn't seem to matter because all they saw was her big nose and fat legs. It didn't matter how intelligent she was. She gives up what she wants in life and trys [*sic*] to conform to the way society feels she should be" ("Comment about 'Barbie Doll'").

The messages about how to be a proper woman start early in childhood and intensify through puberty as girls are made to feel inadequate and as if they can never be good enough. In an essay commemorating the forty-fifth anniversary of "Barbie doll," Piercy reflected on the things that have changed in society since she wrote the poem as well as the aspects that continue to remain relevant, noting: "What has not improved since 1971 is the importance society, men and women themselves, place on body image. In fact, it's gotten worse. The media is incredibly important. We are in a time when people spend hours a day pursuing a perfect body, far more narrowly defined than ever before" ("Marge Piercy's 'Barbie Doll'").

Piercy's "Barbie Doll" has been anthologized frequently, and Piercy has discussed the consequences of the popularity: "It feels as if every class in high school or college that uses poetry reads my poem written in 1971, 'Barbie doll.' I've written over a thousand poems since then, many better than that one, but it's in all the school anthologies and that's the poem they use. The teachers and professors think it's great to tell the kids to ask questions of the poet. I've had 14 queries this week. I try to answer them all but I resent it. It takes time I could be doing my own work."[6]

In addressing issues of appearance and behavior, Piercy has continued to follow the second-wave adage which reminds us that "the personal is the political" (Hanisch). She has insisted that things like who does the housework or the grunt work of organizing, who gets to plan strategy or serve as spokesperson for a cause, are not unimportant issues; they demonstrate male privilege and the operation of power.

In "Councils" (*To Be of Use*), Piercy took on the gendered dynamics of interpersonal communication and proposed new strategies for disrupting engrained patterns. Written to be recited by two voices, denoted by the symbols ♀ (female) and ♂ (male), the poem has the speakers alternate stanzas. Not only is it the woman's voice observing the imbalance who speaks and who is listened to, but also the male voice acknowledging its power and privilege and offering suggestions about changing conversational practices that could mitigate against the deference generally accorded male speakers. Both genders are accountable. Although certainly men are calling other men to change their behavior to avoid taking up more space and attention than is fair, women also have to change their behavior and be brave enough and willing to speak up.

In other poems, Piercy has celebrated the beauty of love and intimacy. "We Become New" (*To Be of Use*) uses images of nature and food to juxtapose the seeming ephemerality and fragileness of a relationship with the solidity and groundedness of it. Piercy doesn't romanticize the difficulty of relationships, especially the difficulty of trying to love wholly, open-heartedly, and in a way that embodies equality.

In *Early Grrrl* (1999), Piercy offered selections from some of her earliest books of poems, as well as unpublished poems written when she was a teenager, and uncollected poems written over the past decades. The collection's title is an intentional reference to the Riot Grrrl movement. In her 2001 interview with Piercy, Michelle Gerise Godwin describes it as "a term used by young, activist women who express their humor, rage, and sexuality through bands, films, and zines—nonglossy, underground self-publications" (28). In 2019, it seems that much of that energy is currently being expressed through blogs, which serve a similar purpose in empowering women to write their own truths without being mediated by the publishing industry. In the dedication to this collection, Piercy "pays homage to all the grrrls whose zines and music and manifestoes I have enjoyed." In her conversation with Godwin, who historicized the term "grrrl" as "a Third Wave term," Piercy emphasized: "I was always a grrrl. I was always blatantly sexual and raunchy" and "I relate to the grrrls of today" (28). The poems in *Early Grrrl* range from existential teen anguish to Piercy's early politicization.

Piercy revisited her hardscrabble childhood in many poems, describing poverty, difficulties between and with her parents, the lack of beauty in urban

Detroit, and experiences of becoming an emerging adult. These poems are set both in present tense and in retrospect. Several of these poems are in *Made in Detroit*—the title of which is a play on her own growth, development, and emerging adulthood—and a nod to the dying auto industry and dire consequences of that death to a highly industrialized city. In "Mehitabel & Me,"[7] Piercy recounts her journey as an author, when she was trying to establish herself as a poet and struggling just to survive. Now, she takes pride in what she has achieved through her work and creativity—economic security and even the ability to splurge a little. Coming from a background of destitution and need, struggling to make her own way as a poet and writer against her family wishes and with little support, she still marvels at what she has accomplished and achieved.

This collection of poems, as with many others, includes reflections on her relationship with her mother. Moramarco and Sullivan point out Piercy's many poems "about Piercy's Detroit working-class childhood, especially family poems about her troubled relationship with her mother and father." Many poems describe a fraught relationship with her mother, especially. In "What My Mother Gave Me," Piercy recognized the lack of beauty and comfort in her mother's life and her mother's thwarted dreams, which impacted the ways she interacted with her daughter.

Piercy also acknowledges her connection to her mother, both in blood and ancestry and in carrying on her mother's dreams. This poem revisits some of the same themes in the earlier "My Mother's Novel" (*The Moon Is Always Female*), where the speaker of that poem describes the similarities between herself and her mother, both physically and emotionally. The mother's desires are stifled by poverty and even when marriage results in a slightly more stable economic situation, it does not provide sufficient scope for to explore her dreams. The best the mother can do is make beauty where she can by, for instance, planting flowers in a small back yard. Piercy noted that she continues to mark "my mother's yahrzeit, the day to say Kaddish for her on the anniversary of her death according to the lunar Hebrew calendar" ("Myths about Cats and My Mother's Yahrzeit").

In all of her poetry, Piercy has written of beauty and grime, of frustration and success, of lovers and family, of activism and struggle—all placed within our contemporary political context and understanding. The poems are insightful, evocative, and wise. Sometimes harsh, sometimes lyrical: they are always powerful.

NOTES

Chapter 1: Understanding Marge Piercy

1. Piercy's phrase is evocative of Virginia Woolf's assertion that "a woman must have money and a room of her own if she is to write fiction" (4). Piercy noted earlier in her career that she has "been very moved by her [Woolf's] essays" (Hamner and Walker 149), but later asserted that "I've never been very engaged with her [Woolf]" (Lyons 336).

Chapter 2: *Small Changes, Vida, Braided Lives*

1. There are many narratives of second-wave feminism available, including memoirs and histories. For readers who would like to know more, see Sara Evans; Flora Davis; Alice Echols; Ruth Rosen; and Gloria Hull, et al. for some examples.

2. The Riot Grrrl movement began in the early 1990s as a response to sexism in the punk music world. Bikini Kill is one of the bands most closely associated with it. Many Riot Grrrls were also involved in authoring zines. See Kristen Schilt for more of the movement's history.

3. See Kathy Davis for an account of the beginning of *Our Bodies, Ourselves* and the ways in which it influenced women's health nationally and transnationally.

4. Piercy was referring to Freudian dogma that for women, an orgasm achieved by stimulation of the clitoris is an immature orgasm, whereas mature women have vaginal orgasms as a result of male penetration.

5. In the 2006 "Introduction" to her 1969 essay "The Personal Is Political," Hanisch shared that she did not create the title of the essay. She believes it was "done by *Notes from the Second Year* editors Shulie Firestone and Anne Koedt" (*Notes* is where the essay was originally published). Regardless, the title/phrase was widely used among feminists and was understood to recognize the term 'political' "as having to do with power relationships, not the narrow sense of electoral politics" ("Introduction"). Megan Behrent has offered that "this insistence on the idea that the 'personal is political' transformed consciousness by insisting on the need to understand the social, economic, cultural, and political oppression of women as the basis for all 'personal' problems that afflicted individual women." It continues to be a useful concept.

Chapter 3: New Histories

1. Apocryphal stories have circulated about Danish citizens or the Danish king similarly wearing yellow stars to demonstrate opposition to the Nazis and support of Jews, but these stories are untrue. The United States Holocaust Memorial Museum provides historical context showing that although Denmark courageously and determinedly

provided support for its Jewish citizens, wearing the star was not one of the mechanisms used. See "King Christian X of Denmark" for details.

2. See Ann Braude for a historical analysis of the impact of spiritualism in the 19th century and its connections to what she called "the women's rights movement" (3).

3. Comstock crusaded vehemently against all manifestations of vice and immorality. He is perhaps best-known for his campaigns against contraception and birth control.

4. See *Iron Jawed Angels* for a version of the fight for suffrage in which Stanton and Anthony are seen as the more conservative activists.

5. Despite this controversy, the *New York Times* obituary of the real Elizabeth Cady Stanton argued that, "the crowning work of Mrs. Stanton's life is held to be by many the 'Woman's Bible'" ("Elizabeth Cady Stanton Dies at Her Home").

Chapter 5: *Fly Away Home* and *The Longings of Women*

1. Piercy also explored gentrification in her earlier novel *Going Down Fast* (1969).

2. Sara Evans noted that "lesbians entered the women's movement only to find that they had to struggle there, too, for autonomy and recognition" (228). In response, "they sparked not only a movement for gay rights but also the development of a self-affirming lesbian culture" (228). As Hogeland described, "the more mainstream women's organizations like NOW experienced a 'purge mentality' in the early 1970s when faced with what Betty Friedan called 'a lavender herring' and a 'lavender menace'" (68).

3. These critiques are similar to those made after the 2013 publication of Sheryl Sandberg's *Lean In: Women, Work, and the Will to Lead,* which was seen as focusing on or relevant to only a small group of high-powered corporate women—primarily those who are white, economically secure, and in heterosexual partnerships. See, for example: hooks, Vara, Bruenig, and Potts.

4. I thank Susan Bickford for this insight.

5. Many reviewers of *The Longings of Women* have noted the similarity of Terry's murder to the 1990 Pamela Smart case in which Smart seduced teenager Billy Flynn and convinced him and two friends to kill her husband, Greg Smart (see, for example: Fitzgerald, Volk, and Wynn). Flynn was paroled in 2015.

6. In "Housewives without Houses," Piercy shares her experience of becoming aware that the homeless are all around us. Becoming "accomplished at recognizing homeless women in malls and managing to engage them" was helpful for her research; in fact, "malls are ideal places for finding the invisibly homeless, the ones who can pass, the ones who pretend to be like us" (42). Mary's experience reflects this reality. She also finds airports useful spaces to camouflage herself.

7. In an early version of the novel, Piercy wrote Mary in the first person, but she ultimately rejected that strategy because Mary "sounded too much like a victim in the first person. That wasn't what I wanted to emphasize" (Lyons 339).

Chapter 6: The Poetics of Piercy

1. Signaling that Piercy's poetry continues to speak to others and be "of use," in December 2016 the poem was sent out to all national and regional council members for the National Parks Conservation Association in the association's holiday cards, presumably as encouragement to continue their conservation work in a potentially hostile political climate. I thank Anne Mitchell Whisnant for this information.

2. http://margepiercy.com/2017/04/16/a-good-seder/.

3. "Right to Life" (1980), by Marge Piercy; from *Moon Is Always Female* by Marge Piercy. Used by permission of Alfred A. Knopf, an imprint of the Knopf Doubleday Publishing Group, a division of Penguin Random House LLC. All rights reserved. "Right to life" by Marge Piercy. Copyright 1980 by Marge Piercy. From *The Moon Is Always Female* (Alfred A. Knopf, Inc., New York). Used by permission of The Wallace Literary Agency.

4. "Ethics for Republicans" from *Made in Detroit: Poems* by Marge Piercy, compilation © 2015 by Marge Piercy. Used by permission of Alfred A. Knopf, an imprint of the Knopf Doubleday Publishing Group, a division of Penguin Random House LLC. All rights reserved. "Ethics for Republicans" by Marge Piercy. Copyright 2015 by Marge Piercy. From *Made in Detroit* (Alfred A. Knopf, Inc. New York). Used by permission of The Wallace Literary Agency.

5. Nuclear Regulatory Commission.

6. http://margepiercy.com/2017/04/10/finally-into-the-garden/.

7. Mehitabel is a reference to two characters created by Don Marquis in 1916 in his column "The Sun Dial": Archy the cockroach and Mehitabel the alley cat. Their stories were made into a musical. In the poem, Piercy relates to the Mehitabel character. For more information, see "Archy and Mehitabel."

SELECT BIBLIOGRAPHY

Works by Marge Piercy

POETRY

Early Grrrl: The Early Poems of Marge Piercy. Wellfleet, Mass.: Leapfrog Press, 1999.
"For the Young Who Want To." poetryfoundation.org/poems-and-poets/poems/detail/47399/. Accessed Jan 2, 2017.
Made in Detroit. New York: Knopf, 2015.
My Mother's Body. New York: Knopf, 1985.
The Crooked Inheritance. New York: Knopf, 2006.
The Moon Is Always Female. New York: Knopf, 1977.
To Be of Use. Garden City, N.Y.: Doubleday, 1973.
"Woman in the Bushes." *Mars and Her Children.* New York: Knopf, 1992, pp. 87–88.

NOVELS

Braided Lives. 1982. New York: Fawcett Crest, 1983.
Dance the Eagle to Sleep. 1970. New York: Fawcett Crest, 1982.
Fly Away Home. 1984. New York: Fawcett Crest, 1985.
Going Down Fast. 1969. New York: Fawcett Crest, 1982.
Gone to Soldiers. 1987. New York: Fawcett Crest, 1988.
He, She and It. 1991. New York: Fawcett Crest, 1993. (Originally published as *Body of Glass.* Penguin, 1992.)
Sex Wars. New York: HarperCollins/Morrow, 2005.
Small Changes. 1973. New York: Fawcett Crest, 1974.
The Longings of Women. New York: Fawcett Columbine, 1994.
Woman on the Edge of Time. 1976. New York: Fawcett Crest, 1977.
Vida. 1979. New York: Fawcett Crest, 1981.

OTHER

"A Good Seder." *Marge Piercy,* 16 Apr. 2017, http://margepiercy.com/2017/04/16/a-good-seder/. Accessed 23 Apr. 2017.
"Active in Time and History." *Paths of Resistance: The Art and Craft of the Political Novel,* edited by William Zinsser, Houghton Mifflin Company, 1989, pp. 91–162.
"Afterthoughts: A Conversation between Ira Wood and Marge Piercy." *Parti-Colored,* pp. 303–27.
"An Interview with Allison Platt of *Sojourner.*" *Parti-Colored,* pp. 175–81.
"An Interview with Denise Wagner of *Plexus.*" *Parti-Colored,* pp. 204–7.
"An Interview with Michael Luzzi." *Parti-Colored,* pp. 141–53.

"An Interview with Peggy Friedmann and Ruthann Robson of *Kalliope*." *Parti-Colored,* pp. 131–40.

"An Interview with *Sandscript*." *Parti-Colored,* pp. 99–112.

"Busy Week, Snip, Etc." http://margepiercy.com/2016/12/10/busy-week-snip-etc/. 10 Dec. 2016. Accessed December 15, 2016.

"Circles on the Water: Introduction to the Selected Poems." *Parti-Colored,* pp. 18–22.

"Comment about 'Barbie Doll.'" *Facebook*. https://www.facebook.com/marge.piercy.9. 14 Dec. 2011. Accessed April 23, 2017.

"Despair." http://margepiercy.com/2016/11/12/despair/. 12 Nov. 2016. Accessed April 23, 2017.

"Finally Into the Garden." http://margepiercy.com/2017/04/10/finally-into-the-garden/. 10 Apr. 2017. Accessed April 23, 2017.

"Foreword." *Lost in Space: Probing Feminist Science Fiction and Beyond,* by Marleen S. Barr. University of North Carolina Press, 1993, pp. ix–xi.

Getting Together: How to Start a Women's Liberation Group (with Jane Freeman), Boston: New England Free Press, 1972. (Also *Getting Together: How to Start a Consciousness-Raising Group.)*

"Housewives without Houses," *My Life, My Body,* pp. 41–44.

"I'm Better as the World Crashes." http://margepiercy.com/2017/02/04/im-better-world-crashes/. 4 Feb. 2017. Accessed April 23, 2017.

"Interview with Karla Hammond." *Parti-Colored,* pp. 23–39.

"Life of Prose and Poetry—An Inspiring Combination." *New York Times,* 20 Dec. 1999, partners.nytimes.com/library/books/122099piercy-writing.html/. Accessed Nov. 16, 2001.

"Living off the Grid." *My Life, My Body,* pp. 47–59.

"Marge Piercy's 'Barbie Doll,' 45 Years Later." http://www.earlybirdbooks.com/marge-piercys-barbie-doll-45-years-later/. 29 Mar. 2017. Accessed April 23, 2017.

"Mirror Images." *Parti-Colored,* pp. 208–18.

"Marge Piercy." *Contemporary Authors Autobiography Series,* vol. 1, 1984, pp. 2267–81.

Marge Piercy: Novelist, Poet, Memoirist. margepiercy.com.

My Life, My Body. PM Press, 2015.

"Myths about Cats and My Mother's Yahrzeit." http://margepiercy.com/2016/12/24/myths-cats-mothers-yahrzeit/. 24 Dec. 2016. Accessed April 23, 2017.

"Our Money, Ourselves." *Women's Review of Books,* vol. 28, nos. 10–11, July 2001, p. 8.

Parti-Colored Blocks for a Quilt. University of Michigan Press, 1982.

"Port Huron Conference Statement." *My Life, My Body,* pp. 101–9.

"Sex Wars: The Writing Of." margepiercy.com/sex-wars-the-writing-of/. Accessed Dec. 17, 2014.

"Shaping Our Choices: An Interview with Richard Jackson." *Parti-Colored,* pp. 40–46.

Sleeping with Cats: A Memoir. Harper/Collins/Morrow, 2002.

"Telling Stories about Stories." *Utopian Studies,* vol. 5, no. 2, 1994, pp. 1–3.

The Cost of Lunch, Etc.: Short Stories. PM Press, 2014.

"The City as Battleground: The Novelist as Combatant." *Parti-Colored,* pp. 161–71.

"The Grand Coolie Damn." *Sisterhood Is Powerful: An Anthology of Writings from the Women's Liberation Movement,* edited by Robin Morgan, Random House, 1970, pp. 421–38.

"The Lunar Cycle." *Parti-Colored,* pp. 59–78.

"The PEN Ten with Marge Piercy." https://pen.org/pen-ten-marge-piercy. 20 Mar. 2017. Accessed May 15, 2017.

"Things Left Unsaid." *Ms.,* Nov.–Dec. 1995, pp. 92–95.

"Through the Cracks: Growing Up in the Fifties." *Parti-Colored,* pp. 113–28.

"Touched by Ginsberg at a (Relatively) Tender Age." *My Life, My Body,* pp. 61–65.

"Trying to calm down." http://margepiercy.com/2016/11/19/trying-to-calm-down. 19 Nov. 2016. Accessed April 23, 2017.

"What I Do When I Write." *Women's Review of Books,* vol. 6, nos. 10–11, July 1989, pp. 25–26.

"Woman on the Edge of Time, 40 Years On: 'Hope is the Engine for Imagining Utopia." *Guardian,* 29 Nov. 2016, theguardian.com/books/2016/nov/29/woman-on-the-edge-of-time-40-years-on-hope-imagining-utopia-marge-piercy/. Accessed Dec. 30, 2016.

Works about Marge Piercy and Other Sources

Abel, David, and John R. Ellement. "Closing Date Set for Pilgrim Nuclear Power Plant." *Boston Globe,* https://www.bostonglobe.com/2016/04/14/pilgrim-nuclear-power-plant-close-may/FRXGHcfMrk3nSngdYueMML/story.html. 14 Apr. 2016. Accessed Jan. 2, 2017.

Ahmed, Sara. *Living a Feminist Life.* Duke University Press, 2017.

Aikau, Hokulani K., Karla A. Erickson, and Jennifer L. Piercy. "Introduction: Feminist Waves, Feminist Generations." *Feminist Waves, Feminist Generations: Life Stories from the Academy,* edited by Aikau, et al., University of Minnesota Press, 2007, pp. 1–45.

Altman, Meryl. "Beyond Trashiness: The Sexual Language of 1970s Feminist Fiction." *Journal of International Women's Studies,* vol. 4, no. 2, Apr. 2003, pp. 7–19.

Andolsen, Barbara Hilkert. Introduction. *Women's Consciousness, Women's Conscience,* edited by Andolsen, et al., Winston Press, 1985, pp. xi–xxvi.

"Archy and Mehitabel." *Don Marquis: Tall Tales and Light Verse,* donmarquis.com/archy-and-mehitabel/. Accessed Nov. 30, 2016.

Atwood, Margaret. *The Handmaid's Tale.* Houghton Mifflin, 1986.

Barnat, Dana. "The Rumpus Interview with Marge Piercy." *Rumpus,* 2 June 2015, therumpus.net/2015/06/the-rumpus-interview-with-marge-piercy/. Accessed Jan. 2, 2017.

Behrent, Megan. "The Personal and the Political: Literature and Feminism." *International Socialist Review,* no. 92, Spring 2014, isreview.org/issue/92/personal-and-political/. Accessed Oct. 25, 2016.

Belfer, Lauren. "Our Bodies, Ourselves: Feisty, Liberated Women Clash with a Religious Bigot in Gilded Age New York." *Washington Post,* 18 Dec. 2005, p. T06+.

Betsky, Celia. "Talk With Marge Piercy." *New York Times,* 24 Feb. 1980, p. BR9+.

Biggs, Mary. "Fiction at the Front." *Women's Review of Books,* vol. IV, no. 10–11, July-Aug. 1987, p. 23.

Biggs. "Mixed Motives in the Antiwar Movement." *Library Journal,* 15 Jan. 1980, p. 226.

Booker, M. Keith. "Woman on the Edge of a Genre: The Feminist Dystopias of Marge Piercy." *Science-Fiction Studies,* vol. 21, no. 3, 1994, pp. 337–50.

Bosse, Malcolm. "A Cyborg in Love." *New York Times Book Review,* 22 Dec. 1991, p. 22.

Braude, Ann. *Radical Spirits: Spiritualism and Women's Rights in Nineteenth-Century America.* Beacon Press, 1989.

Bruenig, Elizabeth. "Sheryl Sandberg's Lean In Philosophy Doesn't Just Ignore Disadvantaged Women. It Hurts Their Cause." *New Republic,* 9 March 2015, newrepublic.com/article/121249/sheryl-sandbergs-lean-feminism-puts-women-issues-risk/. Accessed Dec. 13, 2016.

Casper, Monica J. "Marge Piercy: On Feminism, Politics, and Writing." *Trivia: Voices of Feminism,* Spring 2014, triviavoices.com/marge-piercy-on-feminism-politics-and-writing.html#.WGqLblzMY6u. Accessed Oct. 25, 2016.

Chesler, Phyllis. *Women and Madness.* Doubleday & Company, 1972.

Clute, John. "Seeing the Light." *Times Literary Supplement,* 15 June 1984, 658.

Davis, Flora. *Moving the Mountain: The Women's Movement in America since 1960.* University of Illinois Press, 1999.

Davis, Kathy. *The Making of* Our Bodies, Ourselves: *How Feminism Travels Across Borders.* Duke University Press, 2007.

DuPlessis, Rachel Blau and Ann Snitow, eds. *The Feminist Memoir Project; Voices from Women's Liberation.* Three Rivers Press, 1998.

Douglas, Carol Anne. "Small Change." *Off Our Backs,* vol. 3, no. 11, 31 Oct. 1973, p. 12.

Echols, Alice. *Daring To Be Bad: Radical Feminism in America 1967–75.* University of Minnesota Press, 1989.

"Elizabeth Cady Stanton Dies at Her Home." *New York Times,* 27 Oct. 1902, nytimes.com/learning/general/onthisday/bday/1112.html/. Accessed Dec. 12, 2016.

Evans, Sara. *Personal Politics: The Roots of Women's Liberation in the Civil Rights Movement & The New Left.* Vintage Books, 1980.

Firestone, Shulamith. *The Dialectic of Sex: The Case for Feminist Revolution.* William Morrow & Company, 1970.

Fitzgerald, Nora. "3 Women Are at Crisis Points." *Philadelphia Inquirer,* 27 March 1994, p. B3.

Fitting, Peter. "Beyond the Wasteland: A Feminist in Cyberspace." *Utopian Studies,* vol. 5, no. 2, 1994, pp. 4–15.

Freedman, Estelle B. *No Turning Back: The History of Feminism and the Future of Women.* Ballantine Books, 2002.

Friedan, Betty. *The Feminine Mystique.* 1963. Dell Publishing Co., 1974.

Gearhart, Sally Miller. *The Wanderground: Stories of the Hill Women.* Persephone Press, 1978.

Gilman, Charlotte Perkins. *Herland and Selected Stories.* 1915. Penguin Books, 1992.

Godwin, Michelle Gerise. "The Progressive Interview: Marge Piercy." *Progressive,* vol. 65, no. 1, January 2001, pp. 27–30.

Hamner, Eugenie, and Sue Walker. "Interview with Marge Piercy." *Ways of Knowing,* pp. 148–52.

Hanisch, Carol. "The Personal Is Political." 1969, "Introduction," 2006, carolhanisch.org/CHwritings/PIP.html/. Accessed Nov. 11, 2016.

Hansen, Elaine Tuttle. "Marge Piercy: The Double Narrative Structure of *Small Changes.*" *Contemporary Literary Criticism,* edited by Jeffrey W. Hunter, vol. 128, 2000. Originally published in *Contemporary American Women Writers: Narrative Strategies.* Edited by Catherine Rainwater and William J. Scheick, University Press of Kentucky, 1985, pp. 209–23.

Haraway, Donna J. "A Manifesto for Cyborgs: Science, Technology, and Socialist Feminism in the 1980s." *Socialist Review,* v. 80, 1985, pp 65–107. Quotations from Haraway in this book are taken from the revised and expanded version of the essay: "A Manifesto for Cyborgs: Science, Technology, and Socialist Feminism in the Late Twentieth Century." *Simians, Cyborgs, and Women: The Reinvention of Nature,* Routledge, 1991, pp. 149–81.

Hayden, Casey and Mary King. "Sex and Caste." *Dear Sisters: Dispatches from the Women's Liberation Movement,* edited by Rosalyn Baxandall and Linda Gordon, Basic Books, 2000, pp. 21–22.

Hershman, Marcie. Review of *Vida. Ms.,* January 1980, p. 90.

Hewitt, Nancy A. Introduction. *No Permanent Waves: Recasting Histories of U. S. Feminism,* edited by Hewitt, Rutgers University Press, 2010, pp. 1–12.

Hogeland, Lisa Maria. *Feminism and Its Fictions: The Consciousness-Raising Novel and the Women's Liberation Movement,* University of Pennsylvania Press, 1998.

hooks, bell. "Dig Deep: Beyond Lean In." *Feminist Wire,* 28 Oct. 2013, thefeministwire .com/2013/10/17973/. Accessed Dec. 12, 2016.

Hull, Gloria T, Patricia Bell Scott, and Barbara Smith, editors. *All the Women Are White, All the Blacks Are Men, But Some of Us Are Brave: Black Women's Studies.* Feminist Press, 1982.

Iron Jawed Angels. Directed by Katja von Garnier, 2004.

Jervis, Lisa. "Forward: Goodbye to Feminism's Generational Divide. *We Don't Need Another Wave: Dispatches from the Next Generation of Feminists,* edited by Melody Berger, Seal Press, 2006, pp. 13–18.

Kerstein, Benjamin. "The Golem: Universal and Particular." *Jewish Ideas Daily,* 14 Sept. 2010, jewishideasdaily.com/718/features/the-golem-universal-and-particular/. Accessed Dec. 13, 2016.

"King Christian X of Denmark." *Holocaust Encyclopedia, United States Holocaust Memorial Museum,* ushmm.org/wlc/en/article.php?ModuleId=10008043/.

Langer, Elinor. "After the Movement: Vida." *New York Times,* 24 Feb. 1980, p. BR1+.

Leonard, Vickie. "Braided Lives." *Off Our Backs,* vol. 12, no. 4, Apr. 1982, p. 23.

Loewenstein, Andrea Freud. "Iron-Fisted Fiction." *Nation,* 4–11 July 1987, pp. 24–27.

Lorde, Audre. "Age, Race, Class, and Sex: Women Redefining Difference." *Sister Outsider: Essays and Speeches,* Crossing Press, 1984, pp. 114–23.

Lyons, Bonnie. "An Interview with Marge Piercy." *Contemporary Literature,* vol. 48, no. 3, Fall 2017, pp. 327–44.

Mackey, Mary. "Marge Piercy On Writing Fiction and Poetry." 30 Apr 2015. marymackey .com/marge-piercy-on-writing-fiction-and-poetry/. Accessed Jan. 2, 2017.

Mahan, Meredith. *Notes from an Incomplete Revolution: Real Life Since Feminism.* Bantam Books, 1997.

McManus, Jeanne. "Eating Well is the Best Revenge." *Washington Post,* 19 Feb. 1984, p. 4.

Mernit, Susan. "Suburban Housewife Makes Good." *Women's Review of Books,* vol. 1, n. 11, Aug. 1984, p. 18.

Michaelson, Jay. "Making Men of Clay: Can Imitating God Extend to the Creative Realm?" *My Jewish Learning,* 7 Oct. 2008, myjewishlearning.com/article/golem/. Accessed Dec. 13, 2017.

Moramarco, Fred, and William Sullivan. "'A Whole New Poetry Beginning Here': The Assertion of Gender." *Contemporary Literary Criticism,* edited by Jeffrey W. Hunter, vol. 128, 2000. Originally published in *Containing Multitudes: Poetry in the United States Since 1950,* edited by Moramarco and Sullivan. Twayne, 1998. Pp. 163–94.

Morse, Carmel L. Review of *Sex Wars. Prairie Schooner,* vol. 80, no. 1, 2006, pp. 191–94.

Nowick, Nan. "Mixing Art and Politics: The Writings of Adrienne Rich, Marge Piercy, and Alice Walker." *Centennial Review,* vol. 30, no. 2, Spring 1986, pp. 208–18.

Oreck, Alden. "Modern Jewish History: The Golem." *Jewish Virtual Library,* jewishvirtuallibrary.org/jsource/Judaism/Golem.html/. Accessed Dec. 13, 2016.

O'Reilly, Jane. "Utopians and Firebugs." *New York Times Book Review,* 5 Feb. 1984, p. 7.

Potts, Monica. "Why Do Feminists Hate Sheryl Sandberg So Much?" *Daily Beast,* 12 March 2015, thedailybeast.com/articles/2015/03/12/why-do-feminists-hate-sheryl-sandberg-so-much.html/. Accessed Dec. 13, 2016.

Rapping, Elayne. "Vintage Piercy." *Women's Review of Books,* vol. 11, nos. 10–11, July 1994, p. 46.

Review of *Braided Lives. Publisher's Weekly,* 11 Dec. 1981, p. 51.

Review of *Small Changes. Booklist,* 15. Feb. 1974, p. 633.

Rich, Adrienne. "Splittings." *The Dream of a Common Language: Poems 1974–1977,* W.W. Norton, 1978, pp. 10–11.

Rodden, John, and Marge Piercy. "A Harsh Day's Light: An Interview with Marge Piercy." *Kenyon Review,* vol. 20, no. 2, Spring 1998, pp. 132–43.

Rodriguez, Johnette. "Fighting Words: Marge Piercy's Powerful Poetry and Prose." *Providence Phoenix,* 27 Sept. 2002.

Rosen, Ruth. *The World Split Open: How the Modern Women's Movement Changed America.* Penguin, 2000.

"Roe v. Wade." *Planned Parenthood Action Fund,* plannedparenthoodaction.org/issues/abortion/roe-v-wade/. Accessed Nov. 11, 2016.

Ruppert, Peter. *Reader in a Strange Land: The Activity of Reading Literary Utopias.* The University of Georgia Press, 1986.

Sandberg, Sheryl. *Lean In: Women, Work, and the Will to Lead.* Knopf, 2013.

Schilt, Kristen. "The History of Riot Grrrls in Music." *Feminist eZine,* feministezine.com/feminist/music/The-History-of-Riot-Grrrls-in-Music.html. Accessed Jan. 2, 2017.

Scott, Mark, and Mike Isaac. "Facebook Restores Iconic Vietnam War Photo It Censored for Nudity." *New York Times,* 9 Sept. 2016, mobile.nytimes.com/2016/09/10/technology/facebook-vietnam-war-photo-nudity.amp.html/. Accessed Dec. 15, 2016.

Schroeder, Heather Lee. "Piercy's 'Sex Wars' Links Past, Present." *Capital Times,* 29 Sept. 2006, p. A9.

Seaman, Donna. Review of *Sex Wars. Booklist,* 1 Sept. 2005, p. 7.

Seruton, Roger. "Bodily Tracts." *Times Literary Supplement,* 23 July 1982, p. 807.

Shands, Kerstin W. *The Repair of The World: The Novels of Marge Piercy.* Greenwood Press, 1994.

Shelley, Mary. *Frankenstein.* 1818. Bantam Books, 1981.

Shugar, Dana R. *Separatism and Women's Community.* University of Nebraska Press, 1995.

Slater, Lauren. "Who Holds the Clicker?" *Mother Jones,* Nov. 2005, pp. 63–67; 90–92.

Sternhell, Carol. "Sex, Politics, Vegetables." *Nation,* 24 March 1984, pp. 363–64.

Templin, Charlotte. "An Interview with Marge Piercy." *Writer's Chronicle,* vol. 36, no. 6, May/Summer 2004, margepiercy.com/about-marge/interviews/the-writers-chronicle-interview/. Accessed March 19, 2010.

The Life and Times of Rosie the Riveter. Directed by Connie Field, 1981.

Tobias, Sheila. *Faces of Feminism: An Activist's Reflections on the Women's Movement,* Westview Press, 1997.

Uglow, Jennifer. "Weighing Up the Seventies." *Times Literary Supplement,* 7 Mar. 1980, p. 258.

Van Gelder, Lindsy. "The Jane Collective: Seizing Control." *Ms.,* Sept.–Oct. 1991, pp. 83–85.

Vara, Vauhini. "Sheryl Sandberg's Divisive Pitch to #LeanInTogether." *New Yorker,* 8 March 2015, newyorker.com/business/currency/sheryl-sandbergs-divisive-pitch-to-leanintogether/. Accessed Dec. 13, 2016.

Volk, Patricia. "The Three of Them." *New York Times,* 20 March 1994, p. 23.

Walker, Sue, and Eugenie Hamner. *Ways of Knowing: Essays on Marge Piercy.* Negative Capability Press, 1991.

Walton, Jo. "Living with Our History: Marge Piercy's *Vida.*" *Tor.Com,* 2 Aug. 2011, tor.com/2011/08/02/living-with-our-history-marge-piercys-vida/. Accessed Sept. 24, 2014.

Weinbaum, Batya. "Interview with Marge Piercy, Summer 2001." *Femspec,* vol. 3, no. 2, 2002, pp. 101–3.

Wheeler, Elizabeth. "It's Her Life and Welcome to It." *Los Angeles Times Book Review,* 12 Aug. 1984, p. 7.

Wilt, Judith. *Abortion, Choice, and Contemporary Fiction.* University of Chicago Press, 1990.

Woolf, Virginia. *A Room of One's Own.* 1929. Harcourt Brace, 1981.

Wynn, Judith. "Marge Piercy Tells a Cautionary Tale of Women on the Edge." *Chicago Tribune,* 17 April 1994, p. 3.

Wynne, Edith J. "Imagery of Association in the Poetry of Marge Piercy." *Contemporary Literary Criticism,* edited by Jeffrey W. Hunter, vol. 128, 2000. Originally published in *Publications of the Missouri Philological Association,* vol. 10, 1985, pp. 57–63.

INDEX

CPSIA information can be obtained
at www.ICGtesting.com
Printed in the USA
BVHW070154150219
540338BV00002B/2/P

9 781611 179521